P9-CLD-046

CROSSCURRENTS *Modern Critiques*

CROSSCURRENTS *Modern Critiques*
Harry T. Moore, *General Editor*

Irving Malin

Jews and Americans

WITH A PREFACE BY

Harry T. Moore

Carbondale and Edwardsville

SOUTHERN ILLINOIS UNIVERSITY PRESS

ILLINOIS CENTRAL COLLEGE
LEARNING RESOURCES CENTER

43840

PS
508
.J4
M32

For Jean who helped

FIRST PUBLISHED, MARCH 1965
SECOND PRINTING, JULY 1965

Copyright © 1965 by Southern Illinois University Press
All rights reserved
Library of Congress Catalog Card Number 65-12388
Printed in the United States of America
Designed by Andor Braun

In *Jews and Americans*, Irving Malin has written a necessary, important, and timely book. Mr. Malin is the author of a study of William Faulkner, published by Stanford University Press, and in an earlier volume in Southern Illinois University Press' Crosscurrents series he dealt with the concept of New American Gothic—a book which has been one of our better sellers. In 1963, with Irving Stark, Mr. Malin edited Breakthrough: A Treasury of Contemporary Jewish Literature, for McGraw-Hill. Some of the ideas expressed in the Introduction to that book are expanded in the present volume, which could easily be called Jews as Americans.

Here Mr. Malin not only deals, in its larger aspects, with the subject of American Jewish writers, but he also treats at length the work of seven of them. In this context he is able to present them in a new perspective. I have met five of these writers and have known about half of them fairly well. Half of five?— but we are dealing, in spite of Mr. Malin's usual precision, with some misty border lines, and in considering these men I also think of some other Jewish writers I know. I want to say at once that I've noticed little or no difference between them and other American writers or intellectuals of various kinds. Whatever differences may exist would lie chiefly in their own self-consciousness; to others, they don't seem to possess the mythical Jewish traits. On most occasions they have merely seemed exceptionally brilliant and lively.

The question of the Jewish writer in America receives interesting treatment in Walter Allen's The Modern Novel in Britain and the United States (Dutton, 1964), a valuably perceptive book by a man who, as a native Englishman, knows his own literature well and has, on several long-term visits to the United States, acquainted himself thoroughly with contemporary American writing and its backgrounds. Mr. Allen observes that "in the United States it now seems as though the dominance of the South in the novel has largely passed to Jewish writers, through the best of whose work, the novels of Saul Bellow and Bernard Malamud in particular, a recognizably new note has come into American fiction, not the less American for being unmistakably Jewish." He later says that this new note

> is Jewish certainly but also, one feels, partly Russian. It is not English. Whether it will endure to become a significant conditioning factor in American fiction remains to be seen. But its emergence, after a hundred years of the American novel, shows that that fiction is still a new fiction, capable of drawing upon the traditional values and habits of feeling of the various racial and religious stocks that make up the population of the United States, and capable of sudden growth, development and expansion in directions scarcely predictable.

I wish that Mr. Allen hadn't used the word racial there, for some readers might think it applies to the Jews, and like every thinking man today, Mr. Allen knows that the Jews are not a race. Yet the word is too often used too loosely, like the concept of "Jewish blood," a phrase which inappropriately occurs in Evgeny Evtushenko's "Babyi Yar," intended to be an attack on antisemitism. There's of course no such thing as Jewish blood, any more than there's Presbyterian or Baptist blood. The Jewish heritage—a phrase Mr. Malin often uses—is environmental. Granted, the environment of the Jews, usually clannish, sometimes produces physical characteristics that are fairly recognizable, yet these are intrinsically environmental. The young Jewish men often break with their community, leaving orthodoxy behind, yet many of them still marry Jewish girls, who understand their men's background, their early conditioning.

All these elements have produced some special conditions for the Jewish writer to deal with, and Mr. Malin in his turn deals with the results of those conditions most perceptively. Some Jewish writers don't want to be thought of as Jewish writers, but as American writers. Of course—and that is what they are. It was an earlier Jewish author, Israel Zangwill, who called America "the melting pot." But most of these recent Jewish authors have that previously mentioned environmental conditioning just as a corn-fed author who has broken away from the Middle West has a tempering of another kind which inevitably appears in his work. In a novel that came out after Mr. Malin had written the present book—Saul Bellow's Herzog—the hero suffers from the usual torments of an American intellectual in a country predominantly unintellectual and, in some places, inimicably anti-intellectual. But although Herzog's problems are not specifically Jewish, he does have an awareness of his Jewish heritage, emphasized in the story in certain flashbacks to family scenes, notably in the Yiddish passages; yet Herzog's "alienation" is ultimately not very different from that of most intellectualized Americans. One of the triumphs of Mr. Bellow's book is that he can make his hero the product of a specialized environment and at that same time broadly representative.

I'm not at all trying to say that the Jewish heritage isn't a specific entity—the foregoing has certainly made that plain—but I do think ahead to the time when there will be less consciousness of difference between Jews and non-Jews. Ironically, the vicious political campaign of 1964—still going on as I write this—has helped eradicate some of that sense of difference as, in another way, the 1960 presidential race did in relation to a different problem. In 1960, John F. Kennedy faced candidly the fact that he was a Catholic, and he said with forceful simplicity that he wasn't a spokesman for Catholicism. His election did away forever, let us hope, with one national bugaboo.

In the 1964 campaign, which will be a matter of history when this Preface is read, all the reactionary and usually antisemitic groups have supported Senator Goldwater, and their slander was directed entirely at President Johnson ("corruption in high place") and his running-mate Senator Humphrey ("a dangerous ADA leftist"). The Democrats didn't engage in such tactics, though they did resort to quoting Senator Goldwater's confusing statements, many of which the average American felt were dangerous in the extreme. But the Democrats, heirs of the American liberal tradition, didn't attack Barry Goldwater personally as his opponent was attacked by some of the Republicans, particularly by that model of statesmanship, Congressman William E. Miller. The irony of all this is that Goldwater is Jewish—the native fascist groups that have been so vocal in his behalf naturally didn't introduce this point, though if Lyndon Johnson had been Jewish, America would have had a boiling up of antisemitism of a kind never known before in its history. True, Goldwater is an Episcopalian, but he has what the Nazis (and don't underestimate the neo-Nazis) would have called "Jewish blood." Yet we have seen reactionary groups accepting, even raving over, a candidate of Jewish ancestry—Senator Everett Dirksen in his speech nominating Goldwater kept harping on the poor-peddler grandfather, who everyone knew was Jewish. All this seems to me a victory, however marginal or inverted, for tolerance—if we can have our native-fascist groups supporting a Jewish candidate, well and good. This may help get rid of another American bugaboo. (Irony breeds irony; no sooner had I written the foregoing than Senator Goldwater himself injected antisemitism into the campaign. In a speech at Madison Square Garden, he said, "The Nazi and fascist types—the bigots—are not going to vote for me because my grandfather was a Polish Jew." This bit of imagined persecution was merely a bid for the large Jewish vote of New York City, as the press immediately pointed out. As to Nazi-fascist bigots, Goldwater could only have been speaking of his own adherents—in Germany, the neo-Nazi press had rejoiced at his nomination, and in America it was the extreme right wing—"the Nazi and fascist types—the bigots"—that fervently supported Goldwater, who in his desperation during the last week of his campaign launched imaginary antisemitic attacks against himself.)

That bugaboo long ago passed from literary criticism—the Jewish authors Mr. Malin writes of have been accepted as exceptionally fine ones by the critics, who have no "racist" axes to grind. This also has been good. And Mr. Malin's book, like various essays by Leslie Fiedler and Karl Shapiro—two of those seven writers dealt with at length here—will help clarify issues further. As Walter Allen noted, the Jewish writers have become the outstanding group in modern American fiction—studies of them therefore achieve a particular emphasis. I'm only sorry that Mr. Malin didn't include Isaac Bashevis Singer, whom he perhaps left out because, although Singer is an American resident, he is a special case, a man whose works usually have to be translated, a man who writes chiefly of European rather than American experiences. But he is a first-rate author.

So of course are these seven men Mr. Malin does take up. His own involvement in the subject, as a Jewish writer himself, adds a dimension to the study, and what he has to say about the subject in general and about the separate works of these authors makes his book an extremely valuable one, and a fine addition to the Crosscurrents series.

HARRY T. MOORE

Southern Illinois University
October 27, 1964

ACKNOWLEDGMENTS

THE AUTHOR wishes to acknowledge the generous help given to him during the writing of this book by the National Foundation for Jewish Culture and the National Council of Jewish Women.

Parts of this book have appeared in *The London Magazine, The Reconstructionist,* and *Wisconsin Studies in Contemporary Literature.*

Breakthrough: A Treasury of Contemporary American-Jewish Literature, ed. Irving Malin and Irwin Stark (New York: McGraw-Hill Book Company, 1964) contains an introduction which hints at themes developed fully in this book.

In addition to the sources given in the notes, special acknowledgment is made to the following publishers for permission to quote from the works indicated.

To Doubleday & Co., Inc., for *Summer Knowledge* by Delmore Schwartz; to World Publishing Co. for *An Age of Enormity* by Isaac Rosenfeld; to Mrs. V. S. Rosenfeld for *Passage from Home* by Isaac Rosenfeld; to Farrar, Straus & Co., Inc., for *The Assistant, A New Life, Idiots First,* and *The Magic Barrel* by Bernard Malamud and *God in Search of Man* by A. J. Heschel; to Corinth Books, Inc., for *Successful Love and Other Stories* by Delmore Schwartz; to New Directions for *The World is a Wedding, Shenandoah, In Dreams Begin Responsibilities,* and *Genesis: Book I* by Delmore Schwartz; to Viking Press, Inc., for *The Adventures of Augie March, Seize the Day,* and

xii   ACKNOWLEDGMENTS

Henderson the Rain King by Saul Bellow; to Vanguard Press, Inc., for *Dangling Man* and *The Victim* by Saul Bellow; to Beacon Press for *An End to Innocence* and *No! in Thunder* by Leslie Fiedler; to J. B. Lippincott Co. for *Pull Down Vanity* by Leslie Fiedler; to Stein and Day for *The Second Stone* by Leslie Fiedler; to Random House, Inc., Alfred A. Knopf, Inc. for *Poems of a Jew* and *In Defense of Ignorance* by Karl Shapiro and *Letting Go* by Philip Roth; and to Houghton Mifflin Co. for *Goodbye, Columbus* by Philip Roth.

IRVING MALIN

CONTENTS

Jews and Americans

IN RECENT YEARS Jewishness has become "an eminently marketable commodity." [1] Gentile readers are wildly enthusiastic about *Exodus*, Harry Golden, or *Goodbye, Columbus;* the Jew "moves more easily than he had expected into . . . a position with a Gentile corporation, a Government agency, an English department." [2] It is not surprising that Jewishness is, as Leslie Fiedler tells us, a "passport into the heart of Gentile culture." [3]

But various false images have been embraced by Jew and Gentile. In this respect Harry Golden's work is significant. Theodore Solotaroff offended many admirers of Golden when he suggested that their sage is only a convenient symbol of "togetherness" and folksy wisdom—spurious solutions to tough, immediate problems. Golden is a tranquilizer. "That [his] own 'platitudes and shibboleths' should be as immensely popular as they are is not too startling, then, for they occur on both sides of practically every issue that worries Americans today, without ever disturbing the desperately held notions that our society is fundamentally fine." [4]

Golden does not appeal to intellectuals, but they also find reassurance in Jewishness without really studying it. Many read Buber's *Tales of the Hasidim*

—Norman Mailer discusses these in *Commentary*— but do not read *Trends in Jewish Mysticism*. Although they browse in various high-priced Schocken anthologies, they are unfamiliar with the work of Will Herberg or Abraham Joshua Heschel.

Why is the Jew a new culture-hero? Most answers are insufficiently spiritual. We have our favorite clichés—the "failure of nerve," the "quest for identity" —to explain our plight, but these merely hide the emptiness we feel when God eludes us. We blame Him for not revealing His face; we claim that He is dead. Perhaps the increased interest in Jewishness— unclear and self-deceiving as it is for Jew and non-Jew —is caused by one unconscious need: we are "waiting for God." When we enjoy the schmaltzy anecdotes of Golden, we simply accept "low" religion; when we read about but do not believe in Hasidism, we are equally guilty.

The Jew, whether he likes it or not, has always been "chosen" to bear God's message. He tells unbelievers that He exists. The Jew is respected—and feared. (Look, for example, at *The Devil and the Jews* by Joshua Trachtenberg.) But in America he is unsure of his historic mission. He wants to be accepted by the others; he relinquishes religious commitment for social gospel; he tries desperately to be "natural," not "supernatural"—to use Arthur A. Cohen's distinction.[5]

Thus we have a strange situation: Jew and American confront each other (often in the same person), without recognizing their differences and similarities, their obscure, complex, and mythic identities.

In this book I discuss seven writers—Karl Shapiro, Delmore Schwartz, Isaac Rosenfeld, Leslie Fiedler, Saul Bellow, Bernard Malamud, and Philip Roth— who deal with the Jew in America. They would not readily admit that their art is "parochial," but I hope to demonstrate that there is an American-Jewish context, *a "community of feeling" which transcends individual style and different genres.* Because our writers flee from orthodox commitments, rebelling against the God of their ancestors, they belong to a "deceptive" community; but in an ironic way they mirror their ancestors.

Why these seven? Are all their books Jewish? How can we define their Jewishness? Such questions plague us at the beginning.

The first one is, however, easily answered. At one time or another each writer has consciously faced his Jewishness. (This does not mean that it has been completely understood or embraced.) Karl Shapiro writes in the preface to *Poems of a Jew* (1958) that "the undercurrent of most of my poems is the theme of the Jew, and for this reason I collect these examples now as a separate presentation." His poems reinterpret Jewishness in an abstract way, implying that the "defiance of definition is the central meaning of Jewish consciousness." The Jew becomes "man essentially himself," without any traditional God. Paul Lauter explains Shapiro's stance in this way.

> "Jew" thus becomes for Shapiro, as for Sartre, a reflection of non-Jewish attitudes; the inescapability of being forever a Jew, which Shapiro notes in his introduction, arises simply because in a non-Jewish world the Jew is looked upon, whatever he may choose to become, as a Jew—an atheist Jew, a Catholic Jew, but always a Jew. Jewishness, definable only in relation to its environment, emerges as an "obsession" for Shapiro; never is it an historical and organic mode of human existence.[6]

Delmore Schwartz seems, unlike Shapiro, to be more "favorably" obsessed with his heritage. In such books as *In Dreams Begin Responsibilities* (1938), *Genesis* (1943), and *The World is a Wedding* (1948), he confronts Jewishness "at home," finding much beauty—and terror—there. For the February, 1944, *Contemporary Jewish Record* Schwartz explains his Jewishness.

> I understood my own personal squint at experience, and the fact of being a Jew became available to me as a central symbol of alienation, bias, point of view, and certain other characteristics which are the peculiar marks of modern life, and as I think now, the essential ones. And thus I have to say (with gratitude and yet diffidence because it has been so different for other Jews, different to the point of death) that the fact of Jewishness has been nothing but an ever-growing good to me, and it seems clear to me now that it can be, at least for me, nothing but a fruitful and inexhaustible inheritance.[7]

In his important essay on *The Rise of David Levinsky* (1952), Isaac Rosenfeld writes that he had long avoided reading the novel because it seemed another "badly-written account of immigrants and sweatshops," but when he finally did read it, he discovered that it not only captured spiritual beauties of Old Country (and New)—it compelled him to see that at crucial points the Jew and the American *meet*. The remark is interesting because it informs us that after writing his family novel *Passage from Home* (1946), Rosenfeld could not stop grappling with his heritage. Even when he embraced the pseudo-religion of Wilhelm Reich in his last years, he probably saw in it, as Theodore Solotaroff suggests, a kind of Hasidic vision.[8]

Leslie Fiedler has always been concerned with Jewishness. One of his earliest stories, "Dirty Ralphy," presents his quarrelsome love of the "Law and election." In a review of *Promise and Fulfilment* (January, 1950) he attacks Arthur Koestler's neglect of the archetypal Jew and his journalistic plea for assimilation: The "Judaeo-Christian tradition" needs, I fear, constant transfusions from a living Jewish body, not merely the initial impulse from a dead Savior and a Book. "Roman Holiday" (1954) clarifies Fiedler's positive commitment. The strength of that commitment has led him—unlike any of the previous writers—to explore at greater length all the ambiguities of Jewish-American identity. We see, therefore, his autobiographical essay on "Negro and Jew: Encounter in America," his review of *Poems of a Jew*, his pamphlet on *The Jew in the American Novel* (1958), and his use of a rabbi in *The Second Stone* (1963). Asked to explain the themes in *Pull Down Vanity* (1962), he writes:

> the stories in this book . . . were written over nearly fifteen years—from a point just after World War II to the eve of 1960s. They represent, therefore, various attempts to come to terms with the world of my experience; with the war itself, though only peripherally; the problems of being a Jew in contemporary America, an intellectual and a writer in a society that at once adulates and fears them.[9]

Saul Bellow acknowledges his heritage, although sometimes obliquely, in his fiction. There is Jewish vision in *Dangling Man* (1944), *The Victim* (1947), *The Adventures of Augie March* (1953), and *Seize the Day* (1956). *Henderson the Rain King* (1959) presents a Gentile hero, but in a curious way it is infused with a Hasidic flavor, much like that found in Rosenfeld's or Mailer's later work. Bellow tends to cross genres, and when he writes criticism, he frequently clarifies his attitudes toward Jewishness. In a review of Sholem Aleichem's *The Adventures of Mottel the Cantor's Son (Saturday Review,* May 30, 1953), for example, he writes that "The Jews of the ghetto found themselves involved in an immense joke. They were divinely designated to be great and yet they were like mice. History was something that *happened* to them; they did not make it." This remark appears at the same time as *Augie March,* and it helps us to see that novel freshly. Bellow reviews David Daiches' autobiography, *Two Worlds,* in 1956 and *Goodbye, Columbus* in 1959; in 1963 he introduces *Great Jewish Short Stories,* expanding his earlier comments on Aleichem. It is no wonder that he is so involved with Jewishness because in some biographical notes issued by The Viking Press, he states that at four he had already been exposed to the Old Testament in Hebrew—"he fully accepted the reality of God—but what bothered him was *where* God was." [10] Bellow, like our other writers, is still trying to locate Him.

Bernard Malamud has not discussed his heritage in any nonfiction, but his fiction explicitly affirms his involvement. *The Assistant* (1957), *The Magic Barrel* (1958), *A New Life* (1961), and *Idiots First* (1963) deal with Jews—their election, suffering, and enlightenment—although they express no orthodox loyalties. Malamud describes abstract or archetypal Jews. This is not to say that his fiction is entirely "modern." Earl Rovit maintains, quite correctly, that the tales are "narrated with a discernible echo of the eternal chant, tales of misery, frustration, insensate violence, greed, man's inhumanity to man, and nature's inexorable victory over both the proud and humble flesh." [11]

In a recent symposium on "Jewishness and the Younger Intellectuals" (*Commentary,* April, 1961), Philip Roth admits that he "cannot find a true and honest place in the history of believers that begins with Abraham, Isaac, and Jacob on the basis of the heroism of these believers, or of their humiliations and anguish." The only "connection" with them, he thinks, is by "apprehend[ing] their God." This Roth cannot do. Thus he remains outside of the tradition, although he feels some kinship with Jews, knowing that there exists between himself "and those others who seek his presence, a question, sometimes spoken, sometimes not, which for all the pain and longing it may engender, for all the disappointment and bewilderment it may produce, cannot be swept away by nostalgia or sentimentality or even by a blind and valiant effort of the will: how are you connected to me as another man is not?" Orthodox Jews are offended by *Goodbye, Columbus* (1959) and *Letting Go* (1962), but the two books ask, with varying effectiveness, this significant question.

Granted that our writers have consciously faced their Jewishness (if only to fight or reinterpret it), can we say that *all* their works are concerned with *only* this theme? Obviously not. But once we answer so quickly, we begin to see that different interests may reflect overwhelming involvement. Karl Shapiro, for example, maintains that T. S. Eliot has founded an autocratic religion of modern poetry; *he* must attack it. The very fact that Shapiro describes Eliot as false *prophet* or *idol-maker* signifies an undercurrent of traditional thinking. *In Defense of Ignorance* (1960) is implicitly related to *Poems of a Jew*. Similarly, Leslie Fiedler's myth criticism as represented in *Love and Death in the American Novel* (1960) and *No! in Thunder* (1960) is obliquely Jewish. It is part of his never-ending search for the timeless attributes of God. Although I will develop these relationships in this book, I suggest here that when our writers are *directly* concerned with their Jewishness—reinterpreting the

God of their ancestors—they produce powerful, sincere art; when they are not, they offer less intense, phony, or imperfect work. Roth is weaker in *Letting Go* than "Eli, the Fanatic"; Bellow is weaker in *Augie March* than in *Seize the Day* or *The Victim*; Malamud is weaker in *The Natural* than in *The Assistant*. And so on.

What is Jewishness for our writers? Is it a race, a culture, a religion, or an obsession? Would they accept Sartre's statement in *Anti-Semite and Jew*?

> What is it, then, that serves to keep a semblance of unity in the Jewish community? To reply to this question, we must come back to the idea of *situation*. It is neither their past, their religion, nor their soil that unites the sons of Israel. If they have a common bond, if all of them deserve the name of Jew, it is because they have in common the situation of a Jew, that is, they live in a community which takes them for Jews.[12]

Or would they accept Arthur A. Cohen's statement?

> The irresistible forces of history no longer *compel* the Jew to choose Judaism. In many cases, moreover, he is choosing to repudiate Judaism or to embrace Christianity. . . . It is only the exceptional—those who are searching deeply or are moved profoundly, who ever reject or embrace. The majority tend more often to undramatic indifference—to slide into the routine of the majority without asking questions for which no meaningful answers have been offered.[13]

Any definition of Jewishness for *us* cannot be exclusively religious. We cannot say that *The Assistant* adheres strictly to the Law. But we can begin with the premise that our writers present the Jewish Experience—which is social, religious, and psychological. The center of this Experience is God. Our writers are trying in different ways to discover and name Him;

they search everywhere, attacking pagan deities, and pseudo-religions. In a sacred, paradoxical way they give us modern American views of traditional beliefs.

The Jewish Experience is a series of moments in the search for God.

> Thus, unlike scientific thinking, understanding for the realness of God does not come about by way of syllogism . . . but by way of insights. The ultimate insight is the outcome of *moments* when we are stirred beyond words, of instants of wonder, awe, praise, fear, trembling and radical amazement; of awareness of grandeur, of perceptions we can grasp but are unable to convey, of discoveries of the unknown, of moments in which we abandon the pretense of being acquainted with the world, of *knowledge by inacquaintance*.[14]

These moments are inverted for our writers in that they move *toward* God, whereas for most believers they extend *from* God. Our writers search; their ancestors know. I will concentrate on certain moments—exile, time, suffering, election, and transcendence—which, although I present them somewhat schematically, are meant to be continuous. These moments should be simultaneous, but often they are fragmentary, symbolizing the fact that "modern man has disrupted the age-old continuities of life—religion, the family, the community—and has reduced the individual to a forlorn, fragmentary existence." [15] But the Jewish Experience is *literary* as well as *spiritual*. God has been pictured in traditional ways. Various forms have been used to describe Him: parable (or fable), dream, symbol, extreme statement (or paradox), humor, and prophecy. Our writers employ the same, although for different purposes. Theme cannot be separated from form, moment from word. The Bible, Heschel reminds us, is holiness in words.[16]

I isolate moments by looking intensively at selected

passages, not by attempting any comprehensive survey. These moments are arranged simply. I begin with a traditional concept—say that of exile—and then show how it is modified by our seven writers. My vision is vertical, selective, and biased.

"THERE IS HARDLY a major passage in the Five Books of Moses which fails to refer to and to reiterate the promise that God made to Abraham, that the land of Canaan would be his inheritance and that of his descendants." [1] This classic view is echoed in rabbinic literature: the Holy Land is the navel of the world; its atmosphere makes men wise. But the very existence of the Holy Land presupposes many unholy places where Jews dwell. There is constant tension between Land and *Galuth* (Exile):

> *How shall we sing the Lord's song*
> *In a foreign land?*
> *If I forget you, O Jerusalem,*
> *Let my right hand forget her cunning,*
> *Let my tongue cleave to the roof of my mouth.*
> *If I remember you not,*
> *If I set not Jerusalem above my chiefest joy.*

This disequilibrium introduces many questions which are especially troublesome for American Jews. Is the American as "Jewish" as the Israeli? Should the exile—wealthy and secure as he may be—return to the Land? Does God favor Exile? These questions have been answered in various ways. Mordecai Kaplan argues that "Jews living in lands of freedom are not in

Exile, while maintaining that the state of Israel has a particular importance for a present-day revival of Jewish culture and spiritual values." [2] Will Herberg asserts that "whatever be the particular forms of Jewish existence . . . they are all merely relative, transient and localized; underlying and yet transcending them is Israel as covenant-folk." [3]

What is important is that Exile, no matter how it is interpreted, is a crucial moment for all Jews. Because the Jew recognizes his alienation from the Promised Land, he remains an outsider from his society. The more deeply he embraces the idea of Israel, the more unhappy he is in Exile. It is not surprising that he becomes, in Isaac Rosenfeld's phrase, "a specialist in alienation."

The alienation theme is deeply American. In the beginning the Colonials regard the wilderness as Promised Land, despite many satanic Indians. William Bradford writes, for example, in *The History of Plymouth Plantation*:

> *Our fathers were Englishmen which came over this great ocean, and were ready to perish in this wilderness; but they cried unto the Lord, and he heard their voyce, and looked on their adversitie, etc. Let them therefore praise the Lord, because he is good, and his mercies endure for ever. Yea, let them which have been redeemed of the Lord, shew how he hath delivered them from the hand of the oppressour.* [4]

The special, luminous quality is transformed gradually. America is pictured by the later Romantics not as a Christian sanctuary but as a pure forest. Crèvecoeur writes in 1782 that "*He* is an American, who leaving behind him all his ancient prejudices and manners, receives new ones from the new mode of life he has embraced, the new government he obeys, and the new rank he holds. He becomes an American by being received in the broad lap of our great *Alma Mater*." The transformations continue. Although Hawthorne attacks the Custom House and Melville lashes out at Wall Street, they hope faintly that America can be Promised Land. The modern American is aware of his alienation from holy ground that was (and may be?); he remains suspended. Thus he responds sympathetically to "The Bear" and "Big, Two-Hearted River," finding in them a yearning for the ritualistic sense of place.

It is obvious that once America is *imagined* as Promised, Holy, or Free, it assumes certain mythic burdens. America in 1964 is indecisively "human"; so is the state of Israel. If transcendent America and Israel are placed *concretely*, they disillusion believers. Europeans are disturbed by our country because they have some ideal—now of Pure Violence?—which cannot conform to reality; so are Jews visiting Israel for the first time.

Do our writers participate in the traditional moment of exile? Do they present it only in terms of Israel and America, Old Country and New? Or do they present it as universal, not merely Jewish?

Karl Shapiro is a poet of exile. "Israel" deals with the Holy Land and *Galuth*. Palestine is liberated after so much battling, "starting forth of Feet," and dropping of chains. It lives as a new political reality. But Shapiro—the Western Jew—is uneasy. Should he move there? Can he simply accept the news by sitting in a "Western chair?" Although he is now able to say his "name / Aloud for the first time unconsciously . . ." he cannot completely face his exile. He ends his poem by wishing to "speak the name only of the living land."

Shapiro's indecisive fascination is evident in "The 151st Psalm." (This poem, like "Israel," is commissioned, but it is also private.) Here the crucial phrase is "Immigrant God," which can hold at least two meanings. God is worshipped by the immigrant Jews, or He Himself is immigrant. Both meanings are related: God lives with the Jews. Shapiro seems, however, to run away from Him; he doesn't like being followed. Exile is devoutly wished. But at the same time God's pursuit is necessary and inevitable. The curious psalm celebrates exile from God while affirming that such exile is impossible.

When we look elsewhere in *Poems of a Jew*, we note that Shapiro includes all "works of exile." He associates Jew and exile to the extent that he reprints "University," which deals less with Jewish Questions than with a specific institution. "Jew" is mentioned once—in the first line; the other lines attack the exclusion policies of the university, the snobbism of deans, the dishonest affiliation with Thomas Jefferson. "University" introduces earlier questions: Is it a Jewish poem? Is it a poem of a Jew? The two questions are different. Of course, the poem is not Jewish like "Israel"—it doesn't pay homage to a traditional concept—but it is written by someone who sees the terror of exile—even in social routine. If Shapiro is a Jew only because he is exiled—from what?—then his definition is vague and limited.

The same problems arise with "Travelogue for Exiles." Shapiro explicitly deals with universal alienation. We are separated from "home"; we don't belong to this world—to the heavens, the waters, or the earth. He structures his "travelogue"—there is implied irony in the title; the poem isn't a Hollywood film—by asking about security, meaning, and holiness, and receiving forceful, negative answers. Shapiro is without hope. No orthodox believer could accept the travelogue; it refutes traditional principles because it suggests that there isn't any transcendent meaning to life, except that of exile. But it does "extend" a Jewish moment.

Because Shapiro tends to view exile in universal terms, his work contrasts sharply to *The World is a Wedding* by Delmore Schwartz. Exile is rooted here in the immigrant experience: first and second generation Jews do not know how to cope with their new-found land, despite the fact that it is better than the bloody, pogrom-filled regions they have left. They are engaged in "a bitter farce."

"America! America!" is Schwartz' most powerful version of this exile. The hero, Shenandoah Fish, sits in his mother's kitchen, unable to breathe fresh air; he likes to hear her never-ending monologues. "She spoke always of her own life or of the lives of her friends; of what had been; what might have been." Shenandoah feels strangely at home.

Gradually he discovers new meaning in his mother's stories—especially the ones of the Baumann family. The Baumanns arrived and flourished: Mr. Baumann could sell insurance to other immigrants because "they were able to look down on newcomers to America, and their own early lives in America, a state of being which was expressed by the *word, greenhorn.*" The policies represented security. But the Baumanns could not really adjust to the Promised Land; they repressed their feelings of exile, forcing their children to become their whole world. Dick, a son, was well taken care of—so much so that he could not handle glorious America—let alone himself. He wandered from job to job. The cloying family structure ultimately isolated parents from children, immigrants from land.

While his mother rambles (as do immigrant lives?), Shenandoah sees himself in the family. Earlier he believed that "he was removed from them by thousands of miles, or by a generation, or by the Atlantic Ocean." He exiled himself—or was exiled; he found a Promised Land in his art. Now he realizes that the Baumanns and he are confused because they *imagined* ideals they could not achieve. It is a triumph for him to admit that "he felt for the first time how closely bound he was to these people." The story ends on a more universal note. Immigrant Jews are separated from Old World and New; the writer is separated from his community; "no one truly exists in the real world because no one knows all that he is to other human beings, all that they say behind his back, and all the foolishness which the future will bring him."

Schwartz' early poems, rewritten for *Summer Knowledge: New and Selected Poems 1938–1958*, use a familiar scene—an insomniac pacing the floor or Far Rockaway—to affirm that the "common" is alien. They share a community of exile, maintaining as do Shapiro's poems, that all people are exiled. They are partially "Jewish" because they insist that such exile is a necessary part of life.

"Far Rockaway" describes the seaside resort—"fun, foam, and freedom." Light "sways" and almost bubbles; tired businessmen "loll." Here is the Promised Land. Here is the "cure of souls"—to use the epigraph from Henry James. But Schwartz cannot be at home. These cozy activities are consumed by rushing time, which eats the "heart of man." As men are removed from perfect pleasure, so is the poet removed from the "others." He is "tangential"—a "dangling man." Where can *he* rest? Surely not in Far Rockaway or in his own being. Here, there; "tedium," "blaze"—all he has is a "nervous conscience."

Isaac Rosenfeld's nervous conscience could never rest; it forced him to return obsessively to exile. In "David Levinsky: The Jew as American Millionaire,"

which is very much like "America! America!," he tells
us that he had long avoided reading Cahan's novel because it seemed to be "foreign"—just another "badly
written account of immigrants and sweatshops."
Rosenfeld is surprised to learn that no matter how
"apart" he is from immigrant experience, he identifies
with Levinsky's yearning for Promised Land: "All
things in Levinsky's life are divided, alienated from
themselves, and simplicity is impossible. But no matter how many transformations it undergoes, his hunger
remains constant." This yearning is profoundly Jewish;
Levinsky is "Diaspora Man." Rosenfeld discusses
Galuth at great length because it informs all Jewish existence, not only that of immigrants in America:
"Consider *Galuth*, the Diaspora, through the centuries
in which it has dominated Jewish life: the theme of the
Return, of yearning for Eretz Israel, to which are
linked Cabala and Messianism, modes of prayer and
worship as well as modern political and social movements, so that the whole becomes a compendium of
Jewish activity per se." But Rosenfeld does not stop
here. He asserts that *Galuth* is American as well.
Levinsky is our "typical" businessman who, achieving
success, finds it hollow and wants something more—
perhaps holiness? He is the "poor little rich boy"—a
Baumann who, although successful, is quite unhappy.
Jew and American meet in Cahan's novel: "To be sure,
[Levinsky's] is only a single career, a single example of
the Jew as American, but it draws our attention to the
considerable structural congruity that must underlie
the character and culture of the two peoples."

Although Rosenfeld is concerned in this essay with
literary criticism, he does not always write such detailed analysis. Often he turns to larger problems. In
"The Meaning of Terror," for example, he deals with
universal alienation. Here he tells us that the intellec-

tuals and the bourgeoisie—all social classes—are exiled from any meaning in life. There is only "terror"
because Western traditions—including the Jewish
one—have not been able to comprehend new "model
reality": the concentration camps, the totalitarian
states. Rosenfeld believes that the exile of terror (or
vice versa) stares at him. He cannot get out of it. Like
Shapiro in "Travelogue for Exiles" he sees only this
exile, without any tradition to sustain him.

From identification with Jewish moments to willed
separation from them—Rosenfeld cannot achieve
peace. He is his own "specialist in alienation." In an
essay on Sholem Aleichem he describes the double
function of such alienation: on the one hand, it forces
men to reconstruct the social order, to change; on the
other, it compels them to be so unsure about general
values that it leads them back to private fears. This
double function is evident in the selections I have discussed. Schwartz, Shapiro, and Rosenfeld move from
sympathetic identification with others to weak retreat
into self. They use exile for higher purposes ("America! America!," "David Levinsky: The Jew as American Millionaire" or "Israel") or they cling to it somewhat neurotically.

Exile is the starting point in Leslie Fiedler's work.
He goes to Montana (in an autobiographical essay) to
escape from the claustrophobia of the East—the heritage of his parents? It is a new land—the frontier. But
he discovers that this Promised Land is haunted by
guilt. Montana is really a make-believe place which
tries vainly to match the Romantic view of it, a view
now confined to shoddy Westerns: "The Secondary
Frontier moves from naïveté to an elementary consciousness of history and discrepancy; on the one
hand, it falsifies history, idealizing even the recent past
into the image of the myth, while, on the other hand,

it is driven to lay bare the failures of its founders to live up to the Rousseauistic ideal." Thus no one is comfortable there. Surely Fiedler is not. Surely the persecuted Indians are not. And the natives are not because they believe *all*.

Fiedler ends his brutal essay by suggesting that the Montanan must come to terms with the Indian and himself—both exist in "open-air ghettos"—before he can achieve security and dignity. Exile is a fundamental part of this society—Fiedler says, in effect, that Montana is America—and the Montanan cannot rest unless he knows he lives between innocence and guilt, myth and reality.

"Roman Holiday" is more "Jewish." The title, we soon learn, is ironic—it puns on the concept of fun-filled vacation and serious *holy* day. Fiedler finds it "difficult really to believe in Passover in Rome"; the place is so alien to his heritage, although it "belongs" to the Jews, holding as it does the terrible Arch of Titus.

Fiedler is not at home. He finds that contemporary Jews are so much like Gentiles that he can't tell them apart. The *Seder* itself is a business proposition and a comedy of errors: "It was a completely Roman, non-Paschal meal: broth with pasta, slices of roast veal, and finally artichokes *alla giudea*, which is to say, Jewish style." The Passover reading in the *Haggadah* deals, of course, with persecution in Egypt, and Fiedler notes ironically that because the Roman Jews are exiled from their traditions, they cannot be affected by the symbol of Egypt. Where is he to turn? Is he still a Jew when so many other Jews are "different"? Can the Lord with a strong hand lead *him* to the truth?

The essay ends dramatically. Fiedler and his family meet a Jewish couple—the girl is American and her husband is Italian. When he says a "big day"—that is, a holy day—they respond by talking about the strike. They don't know about Passover! And when Fiedler discusses the strange Seder, they laugh: "Do you mean to say that in this day and age you tell your children . . .—you teach them that we're the *Chosen People?*" Consider the fact that they say "we're." Why do they? Is there, Fiedler seems to imply, something which makes a "we" out of all exiles—those separated from tradition and those separated from assimilation?

Fiedler's fictional heroes are exiles. We first meet Warren in "The Teeth" as he walks to the house in which some female admirers live. Children, dogs, the sun, nameless faces—all "unnerve" him. He believes that he is trespassing; and he exaggerates his limp, feeling at home only in the "tide of evasion and self-pity." Vanity is his Promised Land. The story traces Warren's movements. He cannot be an ideal cripple because he sees a real one who runs sloppily after him. Even when he visits his admirers, he cannot be comfortable; he despises their too-easy acceptance of his myth, his willed deformity. He also runs from them. We see him moving away, "softly, softly." Later he dreams that he can never give up his proud exile—he has nothing else.

Fiedler's stories usually end—as well as begin—with exile. In "Pull Down Vanity" the writer "hobbles down the street, pointing [his] own way home and feeling for the first time that summer almost cold." In "Nude Croquet" we see Molly-o in the "classic pose of nakedness"—alone for the first time. "The Fear of Innocence" presents the hero bereft of any illusions, rushing "home" and wondering what "Home to his Mother's house . . ."—the Miltonic line—means for him.

Bellow also gives us a "dangling man"—a Joseph, Asa, or Tommy. Why does he dangle? There are many reasons, but the primary one is that he is divorced from "conventional" reality because he sees through it. He understands that it is full of *moha*, trickery, and corruption. *It is unholy.* He yearns—as does David Levinsky, Shenandoah Fish, or Fiedler in "Roman Holiday"—for a Promised Land (an ideal construction) in which wisdom and sanctity reign. The tension between Land and Exile can be seen in everything Bellow has written, but I want to look at two novels in detail.

In *Dangling Man* Joseph notes the compulsive way people assert toughness—or as he calls it—"hard-boileddom." Because of this "code," they inhibit "serious" feelings. He does not want to succumb to this madness, but the very fact that he keeps a journal means that he is probably as compulsive as the others. He—like they—adopts a rigid pattern which soothes his troubled spirit. He becomes another Shenandoah, rarely leaving his room. Joseph is, consequently, exiled from the state: the Army regards him as an abstraction—3A or 1A—not as an individual. He is exiled from others—the maid, Mr. Vanaker, his in-laws, and his wife. They have lost their "common humanity," submitting to the "things they lived among." And he is exiled from his Jewishness to the extent that he doesn't mention it—he doesn't realize, ironically enough, that his crisis, his name itself, signifies a traditional moment.

Does Joseph try to find Promised Land or does he surrender to *Galuth?* He muses about the "ideal construction."

An ideal construction, an obsessive device. There have been innumerable varieties: for study, for wisdom,

bravery, war, the benefits of cruelty, for art; the God-
man of the ancient cultures, the ecclesiastic, the despot,
the ascetic, the millionaire, the manager. I could name
hundreds of these ideal constructions, each with its
assertions and symbols, each finding—in conduct, in
God, in art, in money—its particular answer and each
proclaiming: "This is the only possible way to meet
chaos."

The ideal construction "exhausts the man. It can
become his enemy. It often does." Joseph agrees with
Morse Peckham who, in *Beyond the Tragic Vision*,
asserts that cultural history and religion—all orienta-
tions—are rooted in our desire to subject chaos into
ideal constructions, but these constructions may disregard reality:

> Since man cannot deal with his environment unless he
> experiences sufficient internal equilibrium to observe
> what goes on around him, one drive is toward perfect
> orientation; but if he devotes himself too wholeheartedly
> to orientative activity, he will neglect the genuinely
> threatening aspects of the external world.[5]

Most of the characters in *Dangling Man* have sub-
mitted to false "orientation," thereby neglecting their
own "threatening aspects." They have, in effect, killed
themselves. Joseph is torn between the need for construction and the acceptance of rigid exile. This is
why—like the very ancestors he doesn't recognize—he
dangles.

The Adventures of Augie March presents *Galuth*
and Promised Land in a comic way. (It resembles
Sholem Aleichem's work which employs "the humor
of exile"—to quote Isaac Rosenfeld.) All the characters are exiles, but they cannot face their condition;
they find a Promised Land in grandiose scheming.
Mrs. Renling is typical: she maintains that "there [is]

something adoptional" about "larky" Augie—she offers him new clothing, a vision of "holy" life. He battles her.

> But all the same I was not going to be built into Mrs. Renling's world, to consolidate what she affirmed she was. And it isn't only she but a class of people who trust that they will be justified, that their thoughts will be as substantial as the seven hills to build on, and by spreading their power they will have an eternal city for vindication on the day when other founders have gone, bricks and planks, whose thoughts were not real and who built on soft swamp.

Mrs. Renling is an "eternal builder." The juxtaposition of her silliness and Roman greatness makes Augie laugh.

But he is also tinged by lust for Promised Land. Although he wants to rest in his "own specific gravity," sitting in his "own nature"—"free even of [his] own habits"—he begins to yearn for ideal constructions. He tells Clem that he will get a piece of property, settle down on it, set up a home and teach school. He doesn't want the "Happy Isles," he says, but we should not accept his calm statements. Now Augie does want to build something eternal—after rebelling against other patterns, after living in *Galuth*, he wants to exist elsewhere where he can rule. Clem warns him that he wants to become a tyrant. At first Augie can't face his own tensions. After he does, he views his "foster-home and academy dream" more realistically as a "featherhead millenarian notion." He embraces his "larky and boisterous" exile.

Malamud's "Jewbird" has similar tensions. He flies into the "open kitchen window of Harry Cohen's top-floor apartment on First Avenue near the lower East River," thinking that he had finally found Promised Land. But he is rudely shocked. Cohen swats at him—"Gevalt, a pogrom!" says the bird. Most of the dialogue continues this pattern. Schwartz—this is the bird's name!—claims that he is running from all the "Anti-Semeets" in the world who want to destroy him; he wishes only to live in a nice Jewish home. "I like the warm, the windows, the smell of cooking." But assimilationist Cohen hates him because he represents an old way of life, the immigrant experience, which he has tried to forget. And when his son fails an arithmetic test, he forces Schwartz out into the streets, where we finally see him—a "dead black bird in a small lot near the river, his two wings broken, neck twisted, and both bird-eyes plucked clean." Malamud suggests subtly that once a Jew forgets traditional moments he becomes a violent outsider—an "anti-Semeet" of sorts.

We encounter Oskar Gassner, "The German Refugee," sitting in his "stuffy, hot, dark hotel room"—like the Jewbird, he lives in a ghetto. Earl Rovit has written,

> the succession of dark cramped places in which Malamud's characters live takes on symbolic resonance. Caught in a ghetto-isolation without either the liberating fellowship of a ghetto sense of community, or a sustaining spiritual security derived from directed religious commitment, his characters are defined in burdensome images of loneliness—weighed down by poverty, commercial greed and natural calamity.[6]

Oskar is a recently-arrived refugee from Germany who has left his Gentile wife: "Gentile is gentile, Germany is Germany." He is exiled from the Old Country and the New. This homelessness is represented by one heart-rending symbol: he cannot master the English language.

When the narrator attempts to solve Oskar's language problems, he discovers that as a native American, he has taken things for granted. He has not been in exile; he has been at home. But gradually he sees his error. Oskar's exile reflects his own—all Jews are alienated. As the time for the lecture approaches, both student and teacher—the roles are reversed—become tense. They cannot communicate, especially about "free" Walt Whitman, the subject of the lecture.

While Oskar pours his own love of humanity into his lecture by some miraculous act of will, he learns that the Nazis have invaded Poland. The news scares him. But he delivers his lecture—he can speak to Americans!—quoting "And I know the spirit of God is the brother of my own." The narrator feels proud that Oskar is now more comfortable in the new world. The story, however, ends sadly. After receiving a letter from his mother-in-law, Oskar kills himself. The letter informed him that his Gentile wife who converted to Judaism had been killed by the Nazis. America, Germany—there is no cure of souls, no Promised Land—only "open tank ditches" or stuffy hotel rooms.

The refugee appears again in "The First Seven Years." Sobel is a "stocky man, poorly dressed, with a bald head that had once been blond, a severely plain face and soft blue eyes prone to tears over the sad books he read, a young man but old—no one would have guessed thirty." He finds his Israel pounding leather for Feld; he never seems to leave the dark shoe store because he needs nothing outside. Sobel's Land appears, to everyone but himself, to be another ghetto. Even Feld wonders: What keeps him in the store? Why doesn't he leave? When the refugee does leave abruptly, we learn that he has stayed so long because he loves the owner's daughter Miriam—he has worked for *her*: "How strange and sad that a refugee, a grown man, bald and old with his miseries, who had by the skin of his teeth escaped Hitler's incinerators, should fall in love, when he had got to America, with a girl less than half his age." The ideal and exile— are they resolved? Yes. Sobel is told by Feld that he can marry Miriam in a couple of years. Until then he must wait and pound leather.

Exile has been transformed by our second-generation writers. They treat exile as inevitable separation from the Old Country, the puzzling, dubious virtues of "America! America!" It is a social moment. But it is also religious: Shapiro, Rosenfeld, Schwartz, Bellow, and Malamud find little nourishment in the theology of their parents—they assume that the world is often absurd—Jewish religion is not a sustaining force. Only Fiedler in "Roman Holiday" accepts traditional rituals, but even he ends on a note of universal exile.

Philip Roth deals with assimilated Jews who cannot think of the Old Country. They dwell in a "swamp of prosperity" [7]—alienated from traditional beliefs—but they do not view it as a swamp. They worship it: "Possessions have a new glamor. Even burlap has changed. Madison Avenue people tint it and hang their windows with it, so it must cost more. . . . In any case, the hero of Jewish fiction two decades ago knew nothing of Jewish suburbs, country clubs, organized cancer fund drives, large sums of money, cars, mink, or jewelry." [8] Roth's Jews consider exile an "exotic" concept.

But the striking thing about Roth is that although he writes social history, he is obsessed by what Bellow calls the "contrast of spirit and worldly goods." [9] He reinvests exile with religious connotations. He joins Fiedler in "Roman Holiday," Rosenfeld in "The Meaning of Terror," Shapiro in "Travelogue for Exiles" by asserting that exile is not limited to cultural or social displacement—it extends to all people, especially Jews who have abandoned their historic mission. This is not to say that Roth believes in the Lord. He is strongly attracted to Him, but he is ultimately separated.

The displaced person appears in "The Conversion of the Jews." Ozzie Freedmán doesn't belong in his Hebrew school: he taunts the rabbi with such odd questions as: "Why couldn't He let a woman have a baby without having intercourse?" He is fascinated by Jesus—by the miracles which don't fit what he assumes is his legalistic religion. He wonders about the "Chosen People": can the Jews be *more* than equal? Roth makes his hero an exile who tries passionately to find the Lord, even if He belongs to the Christians. But Ozzie, no matter how much he questions Judaism, loves the rituals. When the phone rings during the lighting of the Sabbath candles, he is angry: "When his mother lit candles Ozzie felt there should be no noise; even breathing, if you could manage it, should be softened." What is the source of the boy's anxiety? Ozzie is searching for holiness which is not "contaminated" by human imperfections. He longs for Israel—where everything is pure and divine. He is another "mad crusader" like Fiedler in "Roman Holiday," David Levinsky (as analyzed by Rosenfeld), or Joseph in *Dangling Man*. What is especially striking is that Roth opposes him to the assimilated rabbi. The tables are turned. Who is the real Jew? Who truly understands the tension between Land and *Galuth*?

Perhaps the tableau at the end is too artificial to bear the weight of these questions. Ozzie runs, without really knowing where he is going, to the synagogue roof. There he prepares to—leap into pure, spiritual space? He forces his mother and the rabbi to admit that God can do anything—even make a child without intercourse. He wins his freedom by forcing the others to see perfection. When he comes down into the yellow net, the net glows "like an overgrown halo." Ozzie returns to *Galuth* after his momentary vision.

The tension between Exile and Land is evident in "Eli, the Fanatic." In the very first paragraph we realize that Eli, the attorney of suburban Woodenton, a "modern community," is out of place in Tzuref's mansion. The mansion and Woodenton—these two places symbolize traditional values against assimilation. Roth is deliberately deceptive: Woodenton's stores are "yellow," bright, attractive; the mansion is "sagging" and old. We almost sympathize with Eli when he feels that *Tzuref* is the exile in the modern world. But the attorney feels strange during the interview: the children of this boarding school make him shudder; Tzuref's talk about D.P.'s startles him; and the refugee with the Talmudic hat completely unnerves him. Eli rushes "towards the lights," hoping to be at home. But home is really alien, and in his shaky way, he understands that he does not belong there. Woodenton is no Israel. His wife and friends constantly refer to normalcy or modernity; they refuse to accept mystery—let alone holiness. Eli is caught in the middle; he dangles.

He becomes another mad crusader. He separates himself from Woodenton; he returns to the old mansion. He runs. He cries. He discovers that he is a D.P.—like the "greenie" who screams at man's inhumanity. Of course, he is unbalanced in the eyes of Woodenton: he has destroyed the peacefulness of assimilation; he has broken the circuit. Is Eli crazy or holy? Is he with God or only with his own neurosis? Such questions disturb us. Eli has found (by changing clothes, by becoming, in an odd way, the greenie) that there is another reality. This reality may seem very far from Israel, but in our mixed-up world, Roth is saying, such reality is better than rigid, modern exile.

We have come full circle. Our writers are so removed from tradition that they do not usually see the "mythic" qualities of their heroes. Perhaps they would assert that an Eli or Shenandoah isn't the Jew as exile; and that such identification is at best unconscious. But unconscious identification is the whole point: whether they realize it or not, our writers participate in an archetypal moment of Jewish Experience. Woodenton—America itself—is Diaspora! Where is the Holy Land?

JEWISH LITERATURE often refers to the father-son relationship.

> They asked Rav Ulla: To what point must one honor his parents? He told them: Go and see how a non-Jew named Dama ben Netinah treated his father in Askelon. The sages once sought to conclude a business transaction with him, through which he would gain 600,000 gold *denarii*. But the key to his vault was under the pillow of his sleeping father and he refused to disturb him.[1]

> When a child begins to speak, his father should speak with him in the holy tongue and teach him Torah. If he does not do so, it is as though he buries him.[2]

> Rabbi Hiyya bar Abba did not eat breakfast before he reviewed the previous day's verse with the child and taught him a new verse.[3]

> Said the Besht: "The Lord does not object even if one misunderstands what a man learns, provided he only strives to understand out of his love of learning. It is like a father whose beloved child petitions him in stumbling words, yet the father takes delight in hearing him." [4]

There is honor between father and sons. The father is the benevolent teacher; the son is the obedient student.

The Besht quotation is especially interesting because it reveals the symbolic relationship of father and Lord. Will Herberg tells us that "the affirmation of God as Father is one of the oldest expressions of Hebraic spirituality and it remains the pervasive and underlying conception of rabbinic Judaism through the ages.[5] At first this fatherhood suggested "authority and protection," [6] but these principles later divided: when authority is involved, God is King or Judge; when He offers love and mercy, even to the wicked, He is Father. Symbolic Herbrew religion deceives some into thinking Deity is really fatherhood. It causes many Freudians, for example, to regard God as a superfather, "transferring to the deity the now unconscious images and emotions which in children arose in relation to the father." [7] Herberg suggests, however, that the "very tendency to project the father-image as God already *presupposes* an impulse in man toward the divine and cannot therefore be used to explain its origin." [8]

What is remarkable is that the father-son relationship is rarely hostile. There is little rebellion against legalism. Even when Abasolm attacks David, trying to usurp his rule, his death is mourned. "O my son Absalom, my son Absalom! would God I had died for thee, O Absalom, my son, my son!" But such traditional relationships do not last. It is not my purpose here to explain the reasons for this change; it is evident, however, that our seven writers deal with imperfect father-son relationships in which rebellion supplants acceptance; violence replaces tenderness; and fragmentation defeats wholeness.[9] Thus the father-son relationship mirrors the moment of exile: the Jewish-American family is no longer holy or symmetrical.

Although it is true that this kind of relationship is

modern—as is the moment of exile—it is also deeply American. Goeffrey Gorer has written that,

> [in] some significant ways the birth of the American Republic can be compared with the mythological scene which Freud imagined for the origin of civilization and the institution of totemic observances. In Freud's "Just So" story the down-trodden sons combined together to kill the tyrannical father; then, overwhelmed by their crime, and fearful that one of their number will attempt to take the murdered father's place, they make a compact which establishes the legal equality of the brothers, based on the common enunciation of the father's authority and privileges. England, the England of George the Third and Lord North, takes the place of the despotic and tyrannical father, the American colonists that of the conspiring sons, and the Declaration of Independence and the American Constitution that of the compact by which all Americans are guaranteed freedom and equality on the basis of the common renunciation of all authority over people, which had been the father's most hated and most envied privilege.[10]

Gorer's analogy is perhaps far-fetched, but it does assume that cultures make myths. The father-son relationship recurs so often in American literature that it functions mythically. Consider *Billy Budd:* Billy, the son, "innocently" confronts the law of Captain Vere, his father. Is Billy America and Vere Europe? Is Billy independence and Vere authority? Such questions, phrased somewhat simply, take us to the important relationships in the story. But Melville is not our only writer to deal with the father-son myth. Even less neurotic Ben Franklin tells us in his autobiography that he must exile himself from the commands of his "fathers"—he flees, for example, from his corrupt older brother. Huck Finn, separated from his mean father, is looking for a new one. Nick Adams in

"Fathers and Sons" does the same.[11] So does Willy Loman's older son.

If the American Jew regards the father-son relationship as do the Besht and Rabbi Hiyya, he is probably disappointed by the reality around him—the teenage jungle. If, on the other hand, he cannot accept traditional moments of family life, he is separated from the Bible and later rabbinic commentary. The archetypal Jew embraces the rule of the father; the archetypal American rebels against the father. Two mythic patterns clash: in this clash our writers find tense, symbolic meaning.

In "The Murder of Moses" Karl Shapiro deals with the rebelliousness of the Jews. He tells us that the poem is based on *Moses and Monotheism,* but it seems, again, to be a private one. Moses is an authoritarian father who asks his children to do "impossible" things. The children question the expediency of the flight from Egypt; they gossip about him: Is he really a Jew? Where does he come from? Why does he compel them? In contrast to the tender lessons quoted by the rabbis, the Mosaic ones are brutal and horrifying. The sons hate the father; they express "contempt and . . . boredom openly." The relationship reaches a climax when Moses returns from Sinai with the "stones of . . . law" and scatters his child-like Jews. Shapiro ends his poem with these lines:

> Though you were mortal and once committed murder
> You assumed the burden of the covenant
> Spoke for the world and for our understanding.
> Conversing with God made you a thinker,
> Taught us all early justice, made us a race.

Moses is viewed, finally, as a just teacher.

Shapiro emphasizes the idea of the "murder of Moses." His father is awesome, strong, and alone; he does not expect deviation from his commands (for they are God's)—let alone rebellion. He is a tyrant. Now, of course, this is the Freudian view of the father, but why does Shapiro accept it? Moses seems to symbolize Jewish tradition or, at least, its legalism. The poet fights such commands, wanting to exile himself. But he is ambivalent, especially when he praises Moses for his message of justice. And he makes him sympathetic as well as cruel: "You were simple of heart." The poem presents Shapiro's unconscious ambivalence towards the father and what he represents.

"Messias" echoes these tensions. Again we are put into the mind of the child; the father is seen from afar. The boy is alone in the "darkling apartment," reading poetry, when the doorbell rings. He rushes to the door, peers down the "gilt stairwell," and sees an "old man of patriarchal race" climbing up. The man grows bigger as he approaches; he speaks "the hieratic language of his heart." There is a "black halo" around his face. Here the rhythms quicken: the boy flees from the odd visitor—from the "nameless hurt"; he runs and runs. The man simply sits in the "sacrificial kitchen," and waits for the boy's mother, wanting only a donation for Israel. Shapiro is giving us a symbolic poem. Why does the boy flee? Does he feel guilty because he reads *poetry*, not the *law* of his fathers? Does the old man force him to realize his exile from the tradition? Does the Jew horrify the boy (or Shapiro)? We are not given the answers to these questions, but it is obvious that the patriach embodies the ambivalence Shapiro feels towards his heritage. The father-son relationship turns on the point of law or tradition; it is charged with underlying tension which remains unexamined. Only fright and doubt emerge.

In his introduction to *Poems of a Jew*, Shapiro writes that the word "Jew" retains its "eternal shock."

This shock has to do with "the intimacy of Jew and God. This intimacy is not sentimental; on the contrary, it is unfriendly." Such comments supply the rationale for the two relationships I have discussed. In both the father is "unfriendly" because he is close to God; he has achieved peace with the Father. But the son distrusts or hates his earthly father for this intimacy, and he cannot, perhaps, get to the Father without help.

"Jew" does not give us an earthly father-son relationship, but it views the Jew's relationship to the Father in the same way as "Messias." The Jew bears the "curse" of his name; it is a "blow on . . . [the] heart like a fist." He is a victim of history—of God. The Father, according to Shapiro, has caused this to happen. Why? To compel Jews to follow His law? God—like the patriarchs—is far away (while He is somehow dangerously close). The hostility between Jew and Christian in the poem reflects Shapiro's hostility toward his heritage. *He* is finally alone—without his fellow Jews (his earthly family) or God. But he is not at peace.

In an essay on Delmore Schwartz, Heinz Politzer has written: "Relations with people [in his work] are limited almost exclusively to the group, to the family, where they acquire a grotesque and swollen extravagence." [12] Schwartz is especially troubled by the conflicts of father and son. An early poem entitled "Father and Son" is a dialogue—unlike "Messias" where the father is "removed." The father begins somewhat pompously: "On these occasions, the feelings surprise." He is interrupted by his son who can already tell "the unction and falsetto of the sentiment." The conflict is evident; these opening words merely hide the unconscious hostility. What is the father trying to say? He warns his son to beware of time, death, and guilt—not to regard life as "full of promises." He loves teaching him: it satisfies his own need to expound proudly; it glorifies his hard-earned knowledge. The son is not yet ready to face life with such solemnity; he regards time as a "dancing fire." Slowly he becomes afraid: What can he do? What can he *know?* The father answers: "You must meet your death face to face, / You must, like one in an old play, / Decide, once for all, your heart's place." The lesson is over. The son has learned to be "serious"; he will be "guilty of [him]self in the full looking-glass." There is more sadness than brutality here.

What if the father is duplicitous? What if he doesn't heed his own advice? Is he trustworthy? Schwartz returns often to such questions. Consider, for example, "Prothalamion." The father is pictured at dinner in a restaurant "with his whore"; there he is confronted by the "child of seven years" and his mother. The son learns early that he is corrupt, weak, and self-indulgent. The same scene occurs in *Genesis*. Hershey Green and his mother see Jack Green dining with a whore. Schwartz writes: " 'This hideous scene presents the biggest truth, / Man's Nature is this being-in-the-world.' " Being enacts "Anguish and shame, anger and guilt."

In Schwartz' myth of the family, the son—whether his name is Hershey Green or Shenandoah Fish—is without "correct" paternal principles. He reacts in two ways: he regards his mother as sole guide or he becomes his own father. In either choice there is what Politzer has called "grotesque and swollen extravagance." Thus when Schwartz gives us Shenandoah Fish in "America! America!" or Seymour in "The Child is the Meaning of this Life," we sense that the lonely son is odd—he is less interested in life than in his closeness to his mother. He sits with her; he has turned completely inward. Shenandoah returns from Paris in 1936 and stays at home, unable to renew old friendships. He "takes it easy," drifting into an indolent, comforting pattern. Only when he forces himself to explore his motives, does he remember that he has an identity apart from that of his mother. Seymour is not as creative as Shenandoah. He almost merges completely with his generous mother. "His mother spoiled him as never before, she was undisturbed when he lost or quit his jobs, and she never disturbed him when he slept late in the morning." He is at ease with other children whom he can tease or impress. Of course, when his mother is dying, he panics. Both sons hate their mothers—while they love them. They smile at their stories, lessons, and habits—this is the only way they can avoid hating their own submission.[13]

The adult as child—this is Schwartz' understanding of immigrant Jews. In perhaps the most dramatic moment of "The Child is the Meaning of this Life" Jasper visits his grandmother in the hospital and suddenly perceives the meaning of family life—"the history of his family arose, illuminated, in his mind, as if he had entered a house at night and turned on the light in each room, and looked at the things which had long been there, but which he saw as if for the first time." Seymour was made unnatural by his closeness to the mother; so were Rebecca and Nancy. But Jasper (regarding his aunt, mother, and uncle) knows that *he* views "the adult world as he had had to look at his mother"—his entire interpretation is probably distorted. This final understanding cleanses him, but it doesn't *save* him. A middle-aged man (the symbolic father?) waiting for a taxi, asks him: "Do you have a light?" All Jasper can say is "No, I have no light." He remains in darkness.

Passage from Home, Isaac Rosenfeld's only published novel, deals with similar tensions; again the father-son relationship mirrors the loss of traditional, natural values. The narrator, Bernard, remembers his fourteenth year when he seemed, at first, to "[tower] over life." He learns that he cannot really tower over life because he has not yet confronted his father and what he symbolizes—he has not yet made his passage from home.

Bernard's father does not like to believe that his shaky rule is disappearing. He pesters his son (and everyone else); he is full of "unwarranted rage." But he is not strong enough to admit that he cares less about others than himself—he zealously guards what little humanity he owns, thereby growing smaller in his son's eyes. Bernard suffers from having a "missing" father—a poor teacher. But he is less isolated than Shenandoah Fish because he adopts a new father in Cousin Willy who, he tells us, "was not only no cousin—he was no Jew. Strictly speaking, he was a hillbilly; born in the Tennessee hills, he had lived South, lived West, been a miner, a newspaperman, a sailor, and had seen the world. I really do not know what he was doing among us." Willy supplants the real father. He offers kindness, vivacity, and happy irresponsibility. He is an attractive symbol of the Gentile world that exists outside of the home. Even Willy, however, is far from perfect—he is also strangely immature.

Bernard is trapped between two childish fathers. He longs to become better than either one—to become his own father. He devises a method to gain a new family; he will marry Willy and Minna, his stern aunt! If he can create this situation, he will declare his own mastery over people. Such precocious planning—such serious play—is at the heart of the novel. Bernard has the two meet, preparing each to face the other; he even lives with them, rejecting the mess at home. And yet despite his maneuvering, the marriage never occurs: Minna is already married; Willy cannot gain maturity; and Bernard understands that, in effect, he wants Minna for himself. His earlier insight is painfully confirmed. "I felt the complexity of things. I would dream of a simple world, of simple motives and emotions; but the world I knew was so complex that no knowledge was without a trace of disappointment. For my pleasure lay only in anticipating, in wondering whether I could foretell that which, when it occurred, would leave me feeling both surprised and cheated."

Because his "new existence" has failed—it has been neither free nor exciting—Bernard returns home, aware that he has never really left it. Rosenfeld does not give us the happing ending—the prodigal son is not received joyously. His father merely says, "So you're back." Later when time comes for the lesson, they take up their "accustomed positions." The father sits in "partial shadow. He would lose feature and personality and, no longer himself, would become mere and absolute father, an image at the periphery, never clearly seen." Bernard has nothing to say when he is questioned about his passage. He only makes his father guilty about *his* flight with Minna many years ago. Guilt *momentarily* unites them: "My only hope had been to confess that I did not love him, to admit I had never known what love was or what it meant to love, and by that confession to create it. Now it was too late. Now there would only be life as it came and the excuses one made to himself for accepting it."

In his literary criticism Rosenfeld constantly discusses "character." He attacks flatness, artificiality, and cliché-language—those qualities which result from non-acceptance of the human. As Theodore Solotaroff writes: " 'Character'—whether in the conventional literary sense or as the writer's self-portrayal—was for Rosenfeld not only the essential element of fiction but also the most telling index of the writer's intelligence and passion, his capacity for understanding and judging the world." [14] Such concern is related to Rosenfeld's search not only for love but for authority. (Can the two be separated?) It results from the kind of father-son relationship in his autobiographical *Passage from Home*.

"Gandhi: Self Realization Through Politics" demonstrates Rosenfeld's desperate need to explore the nature of greatness. Gandhi emerges as a true spiritual father; he contains and triumphs over contraries. Perhaps his most interesting motivation is his wish to regard himself as murderer of his father. "On the night of his father's death young Gandhi, relieved by his uncle, went straight to the bedroom to have intercourse with his wife, who to his double shame, was pregnant with their first child. Father Gandhi died while they were having intercourse." When we look at Rosenfeld's autobiography (as reflected in his novel), we realize that he finds Gandhi fascinating because he is also separated from the father. But Gandhi becomes his own father, achieving integrity and authority after defeating his guilt-ridden egotism. "It is precisely this in which Gandhi's greatness lies, and in which he has few peers: that he performed a basic operation on life, converting everything natural to the ideal with such success that in his case one must almost create a special category—this life of artifice and regulation by the will represents a new species of nature." And did not Bernard seek this "new species of nature" and fail to find it? His alter-ego, Isaac Rosenfeld, *does*—not in the Jewish father but in an Indian ascetic.

The Fiedler hero is a lonely son baffled by the "fathers" around him: unsure of his position in the world, he does not know whether to be vain, arrogant, condescending, or afraid. He is obsessed, in other words, with the nature of authority: Can he survive? Can he become a *Mensch?* Can he find in Jewish tradition some sustaining, paternal force?

An early story, "Dirty Ralphy," presents the fearful son. His father commands him to fight for Truth—to lash out at the anti-semitic boys in the neighborhood—but he is too weak to obey him. Rather, he thinks in symbols: Ralphy, the "Gentile" bully, becomes "the extreme revelation of what awaited those who, outside our Law and election, began by not washing their hands, and plunged through extravagance, poor diet and dirtiness toward final depravity." The boys finally fight; Ralphy wins. What is especially interesting is that the story is a reminiscence; many years later the boy, now a man, returns to the scene. He learns to his amazement that Ralphy was Jewish! His memory has been duplicitous. Although he still thinks in symbols, he fails after this revelation to consider the value of his father's commands. Why did he once fight? To satisfy *him.* But what did *he want?* There is no resolution in the story; it is haunting because it does not deal with the real conflict—between fearful son and "mean" father—but it suggests a pattern which appears in later stories.

In "Nobody Ever Died from It" Hyman Brandler, at thirty-five, remembers his job as a shoe salesman. At fourteen he worked with an obscene, vulgar, Jewish homosexual named Abie Peckelis, who functioned as his father, instructing him in the ways of the world. He clowned with shy women; he taught his "son" to be generous and compassionate. At a Christmas party Abie did a Jewish dance with Murphy, the cop; he ridiculed himself—and everyone? He demonstrated the failure of his life. Why does Hyman *now* remember such a grotesque incident? He knows, as does the adult narrator in "Dirty Ralphy," that he has betrayed a good teacher; he has been false—like all the rest—to Abie, not recognizing his wisdom—his insights into the absurd dreams we all have. "Middle-aged" Hyman is a failure—to himself and his father-image. He cannot write; he dangles childishly.

Hyman appears again in "An Expense of Spirit," repeating that he does not completely fit in the store, "one of the smallest on a second-rate business street," where he clownishly sells shoes. He is still a writer, although an unpublished one. His only home is the library; here he is safe and "different"—"not my father's son, but my own creation." This statement is especially revealing because it shows us that his failure (to please the father?) is over-compensated by self-creation—by rebirth. But Hyman cannot achieve his own fatherhood—his own divinity?—as long as he lacks an ideal figure to emulate and surpass. Unconsciously, he seeks the father so that by destroying him he can reign alone. At one point he admits that "the examining psychiatrist told me . . . that I *want* the limp, that I cling to it as at once a kind of revenge against my father and a punishment of myself."

Hyman meets Noel (and his wife) during a Great Books discussion. This braggart is proud of his strength and good-will. He is, in an odd way, a father-image—as was Abie Peckelis; he *adopts* Hyman without his permission. There is, however, one deep scar in Noel's booming health. When he cannot fight some hostile teenagers who taunt him, he collapses, realizing that he is an old man or possibly, even worse, a "fairy." Thus Hyman is shocked. He is free once more from the clutches of the false father—as in the previous story—but he has not yet learned the truth about human frailty. He does not see himself in Noel; he does not "identify" with him—as does Bernard with his father. The only thing he acquires from the entire incident is Noel's denture, which falls to the ground. It "is, besides a trophy and a warning, an unflagging joke, quite real though difficult to define." It holds unexamined truths.

When we look at Fiedler's criticism, we see that it lashes out at the "authorities." It refuses to adopt conventional tones or concerns. It destroys the old images (even of the New Critics' "pure" readings) in a moralistic, personal way, maintaining—as would a mature Hyman?—that "the image of man in art, however magnificently portrayed—indeed, precisely when it is most magnificently portrayed—is the image of a failure. There is no way out." Fiedler's rebelliousness arises from the need to battle the "fathers" (who have proven false) and to become his own self-creation.

Not only does his criticism adopt an "improper," boyish tone—it deals thematically with its own boyishness. An essay like "No! in Thunder" suggests that the great works of literature are negative in that they confess "the inevitable discrepancy between dream and fact, between the best man can imagine and the best he can achieve." (Remember the essay on Montana!) Fiedler implies that these great works mirror, in effect, his own criticism and fiction. When he discusses *specific* themes—not a general view of "negative thinking"—he is also circling back upon himself. For example, he is concerned in both *No! in Thunder* and *Love and Death in the American Novel* with the "eye of innocence"—the child in literature. I do not want to explore the many meanings he gives to the child as myth, but it is obvious that this figure reflects the fictional Hyman. When Fiedler writes that the "child remains still, what he has been since the beginnings of

Romanticism, a surrogate for our unconscious, impulsive lives," his statement suggests not only his preoccupation with Hyman's role but with his own. Fiedler's son-figures are projections of his necessary liberation from the father.

And this explains a related theme. Many people were (and still are) disturbed by his discovery of latent homosexuality in children's classics—*Huckleberry Finn*, *Moby Dick*, and *The Leatherstocking Saga*. It is clear that when Fiedler discusses these books, he is concerned not so much with sex but with correct authority—fatherhood. *His* Jim and Huck are really communicative father and son. Their relationship is an ideal one, unlike the fragmented ones of Hyman and Noel or Hyman and Abie. It exists "out of time"—in a Promised Land. It cannot be achieved again because it is "too good to be true."

It may be a long way from an interpretation of *Huckleberry Finn* to Jewishness, but Fiedler knows that literary criticism—like religion—must deal with archetypal responses to spiritual crises. The father-son relationship occurs so often in all his work that we can assume it mirrors his own involvement with patriarchs and the Father. (Of course, such assumption is dangerous because it fails to isolate *beginnings* of the pattern.) And in one essay, "Roman Holiday," we see that he (as "fictional character") does *openly* associate fatherhood with Jewish tradition. Here he is the father who wants to bridge the gap between generations—as does Hyman, the son—so that he can teach his sons about traditional Jewish experience. Again the father-son relationship is not ideal—it is inevitably broken. Fiedler cannot be either a patriarch or uncertain son. Benjamin De Mott has written: "His main subject is not fear of sex but fear of the loss of humanity, the self, wholeness. At the heart of the myth that he dislodges, you encounter a human figure afraid of losing either his right or his capacity to speak out of the center of his being." [15] This figure is the exiled son—the Jew—uncertain of his place in the world, approaching and retreating from "fathers."

Saul Bellow's novels deal with the same kind of father-son relationship. I want here to concentrate on one novel, *The Victim*. In it we meet similar archetypes: the tyrannical, false father (Bernard's father or "Messias") the "ideal" father (a comic Noel or Gandhi), and the ambivalent son.

The novel itself introduces us to a world of men— women are not very important. Asa Leventhal, like Joseph, is a "bachelor"; his wife, Mary, has gone to visit her family. He finds himself in "care" of his nephew—the sick son of Elena and Max, his missing brother. Mickey becomes his charge—symbolically he resembles Asa because they are both "victims" of some "chance" process. The sick son makes him think: "Should someone else—he thought of it seriously— have the right to take the child away? . . . Well, that was the meaning of helplessness." Asa also becomes the father of Philip, Mickey's brother. He decides that the boy should spend some time with him in Manhattan. He identifies with this victim, finding in him "something in common." But the "confidence in the understanding between them" fades: "I'm out of touch with kids." Philip is too young to understand the haunted thoughts of his father. When Max returns after Mickey's death to reestablish himself as a responsible parent, Asa instructs him, even though "they never, since childhood, spent an hour together." He says: Children must be protected. "They were mauled in birth and they straightened as they grew because their bones were soft. Mauled again later, they recover again." Max—like a child—must be taught to protect himself. Why does Asa deliver this lengthy sermon?

He is a helpless son, alone in a world of tyrannical fathers. We see him in the office at the "mercy" of Mr. Beard and the others who have power and influence. He is somewhat afraid to leave the office for his Staten Island trip. He has always been dependent upon "business fathers": Williston, Harkavy, Dunhill (who sells him the ticket). Occasionally, he rebels against them, but the rebellion—like Joseph's fits of violence—is blind. Thus with Rudiger he claims that outsiders haven't a chance for decent jobs because the guild runs everything. He "stands up" to him, ranting for his rights—unaware of his real motives.

Kirby Allbee is, of course, his most important adversary. He is "paternal" because he holds all the authority—even though he seems weak—which Asa fears (and wants—witness his guidance of Mickey, Philip, and Max). He represents, in an ambiguous way, the conscience—the superego. His tales about Rudiger are designed to make Asa suffer with guilt. "I say you're entirely to blame, Leventhal." He forces him to acknowledge the "sanctity of the insulated and injured"—to see his own sinful helplessness.

If Asa is torn by ambivalence, he "loves" Allbee as he "hates" him because the tyrannical father is what he wants to be—at least partially. Consequently, his reactions toward him are confused, misdirected, odd. "Illness, madness, and death were forcing him to confront his fault." The following passage effectively captures his ambivalence.

> But suddenly he had a strange, close consciousness of Allbee, of his face and body, a feeling of intimate nearness such as he had experienced in the zoo when he had imagined himself at Allbee's back, seeing with microscopic fineness the lines in his skin, and the smallest of his hairs, and breathing in his odor. The

same sensations were repeated; he could nearly feel the weight of his body and contact of his clothes.

Despite the fact that the passage stresses physical details, it does not suggest latent homosexuality so much as the power-weakness of Asa who, like all of Bellow's sons, cares more about will than sex. He "respects" Allbee for torturing him; he likes the tyrant because he shows him that *someone can rule the world*. There is one incident, however, which forces Asa to strike out at his father. (It is the most dramatic one in the entire novel.) He returns to his apartment to find Allbee, "naked and ungainly," standing beside a woman who is dressing in haste. I think Asa is upset not only because Allbee has defiled the "marriage bed," but also because he has been "untrue": Allbee has slept with a woman! The act violates their eternal bond—sex corrupts the "will to power."

We don't get a picture of Asa's real father—there are only hints to suggest his personality. This lack of development limits the novel. Surely we need to know more about him so that we can understand the hero's odd relationships. I agree with Richard Chase in this respect.

What is so far chiefly missing in Bellow's writing is an account of what his heroes want to be free *from*. As Bellow is always showing, their very adaptability lays them open to forms of tyranny—social convention, a job, a father, a lover, a wife, their children, everyone who may want to prey upon them. And all of these forms of tyranny, fraud, and emotional expropriation Bellow describes brilliantly. But only in *Seize the Day* is there a fully adequate dramatically concentrated image of what the central figure is up against—the institutional, family, and personal fate that he must define himself by, as heroes in the greatest literature define themselves.[16]

The dead father—society's "representative"—is almost too frightening for Asa to face. But he should face him. So should Bellow.

Here are some passages which describe the dead father. We are told that he owned a small drygoods store. He was a "turbulent man, harsh and selfish toward his sons." Later Asa repeats the same information, calling his father a "stern, proud old fool with his savage looks, to whom nothing mattered save his advantage and to be freed by money from the power of his enemies." These thoughts pain him; he tries to stop thinking. But incidents keep his memories alive. He remembers, for example, his father's remark about the many deaths of foreign children. These hints are all we know—they are insufficient to explain Asa's actions in any complete way; however, they indicate that he has never come to terms with authority. Asa is ambivalent: he calls his father "stern" and "proud," but *he* would like to have these qualities—and the mess in which he finds himself forces him to see that some pride or sternness would help. The ambivalence he has always felt toward his father colors his reactions toward the other males in the novel—his "paternal" affection for Philip and Max; his "filial" tensions toward Allbee.

It is characteristic of Bellow to introduce an ideal father who tries to help the son adjust to the world. Sometimes the spiritual guide is tricky. But his "corruption" is less tyrannical than the gleeful authoritarianism of an Allbee. In *The Victim* Schlossberg is the spiritual guide who, in teaching Asa, offers Bellow's message. This "large old man with a sturdy gray head, hulking shoulders, and a wide, worn face" compels Asa to be "strongly drawn to him." The attraction is increased when Schlossberg gives his sermon on the "exactly human" principle. Asa learns from his guide that we should be firm—we should not be humble one day and proud the next. "Choose dignity." Of course, the message is a bit superficial, but Asa follows the "spirit," not the "law."

The Victim "resolves" the father-son relationships. Asa does choose some degree of dignity: he accepts his guilt (everyone's guilt) for Kirby Allbee's failures; he understands the reasons for his twisted involvement with authoritarian figures. But the solution to his problems is "lucky." Can he really escape from the dead father? Can he really meet an ideal guide? Such questions trouble us. Perhaps the false tone is generated fully at the end of the novel: Asa, we discover, will be a father in a month—Mary is pregnant. Things will work out well for the family. But I suspect that his ambivalence towards authority will continue to trouble Asa as a parent. That, however, is another novel—one Bellow has not *written yet.*

Bernard Malamud returns us to the traditional father-son relationship. In *The Assistant* Morris Bober mourns his son, "gone so long from him." Before he can fall asleep he must think of his "form and image." Although he has his wife and daughter, he cannot stop thinking about the past. The past and Ephraim—these two "forms" dominate his unhappy, claustrophobic existence. Thus Morris is an interesting foil to most of the tyrannical, uncertain fathers we have met: he is, strangely, an "old wise man" who has no one to teach or to console. He is unconsciously looking for a son.

It is ironic that he is forced into the position of adopting (or being adopted by) Frank Alpine. Frank is a Gentile—an outsider who, presumably, has nothing to learn from him—and a criminal. Surely, Malamud wants us to accept the fact that there cannot be blood ties between them; and then he forces us to contradict our previous assumption. Frank is an orphan—he seeks a father and finds him in St. Francis, "a great man" with the "nerve to preach to birds." But somehow this ideal is not as effective as "real" Morris. Frank wants to atone for stealing from him, to beg forgiveness of his new father. When they meet, they "break bread"—a communion which transcends religious boundaries. From this ritualistic act father and son are attracted to and repelled by each other. Frank admits, "What I mean to say is that when I need it most something is missing in me, in me or account of me." He wants to complete himself. How can he? At times he fights the grocer because he does not seem to be like him—the Jew bothers him! His guilt gets in the way of "experience." And Morris is exiled from his monkish son because he has been so accustomed to derision that he cannot tolerate goodness in others—especially in Gentiles. There is a spiritual dance encompassing exile and togetherness.

The two partners draw closer unwillingly, until they are one. This union results from suffering which lifts them out of their usual roles and transforms them. In a lengthy conversation—or lesson—Frank and Morris discuss Jewish identity. The Jew, Morris says, believes in the Law. "This means to do what is right, to be honest, to be good. This means to other people. Our life is hard enough. Why should we hurt somebody else?" He continues to state simply, "I suffer for you." Morris' capacity as *Jew* to endure suffering for others, compels Frank to realize that *he* suffers for the old man. Father and son lose their identities; they are Jewish—human. The change is symbolized in a simple way. Frank becomes Morris (after the grocer dies). He jumps into his grave; he continues to work in the store; he provides for the other Bobers; and he confirms his conversion by having himself circumcized. Jonathan

Baumbach writes: "In continuing Morris' life, Frank fulfills the possibilities of the grocer's actual son, the son who died while still a child. It is the least Frank can do for the man he has wronged, and the most." [17]

Many of Malamud's stories echo this transcendent relationship. "Idiots First" opens with Mendel, the father, sighing "Isaac" for his son with the "astonished mouth" and thick gray hair. Father and son communicate easily, discussing food, shelter, and sleep—necessities. They respond "naturally" without any need to engage in lengthy conversations or neurotic introspection. They know "what it means—human." But their humanity co-exists with cosmic law which Malamud, interestingly enough, represents by another father-image—Ginzburg. Ginzburg wants to "adopt" Isaac, to lead him to death. He miraculously appears to block close happiness. When he and Mendel argue about this helpless son, they remind us of Satan and God discussing Job. Isaac is saved at the last minute—as is Frank Alpine—through the good father's sympathetic intervention. He leaves for California; Mendel waits for Ginzberg to take *him*.

In a less successful work, "Suppose a Wedding," Feuer counsels his daughter to marry Ben, the writer, rather than Leon, the "store owner from Newark." (Ben and Leon reflect Jacob and Esau fighting for their father's birthright.) He teaches Leon, "Do you really know the condition of human existence? Do you know what the universe means? I'm not talking about who's dead but also about millions of people—in the millions—who live for nothing." He wants him to face pain and suffering. But Leon responds in clichés. "I feel a catharsis through pity and terror." Feuer is dissimilar from Malamud's other fathers because he realizes that he is to blame not for Leon but for the problems of his own wife and daughter. He is mischievious and sinful—more complex than Morris or Mendel. But he still triumphs over the situation: he compels Leon to leave—at least "today"—and Ben to arrive "early." He supposes a wedding.

In *A New Life* Malamud presents a confused "orphan" (like Frank) who battles the fathers around him. The setting is academic but the figures are mythic.

When we first meet S. Levin he has arrived in "a strange land"—Marathon, Cascadia. He is an awkward, childish, and lonely bachelor. He cannot cope with family-life: the tuna fish, children urinating. Levin at first heeds the advice of Dr. Gilley, his new "father," who instructs him in the ways of the academic world. Gilley is another of Malamud's good fathers—at least on the surface. We expect, from the first chapter, the same kind of father-son relationship we find in *The Assistant*. But the matter is complicated by Pauline, Mrs. Gilley, who is the mother-wife figure. There is a triangle here instead of the usual parallel lines.

Throughout his "new life" Levin cannot adjust because he is attracted to the "family"—to the authority of Dr. Gilley and to the beauty of Pauline—and repelled by it, realizing that if he reaches for beauty he fights law. He cannot question others; he remains alone. What can this insecure son do? He *drifts* into rebellion against the father. Levin sees that Gilley is a sneak, not a correct master, and that family life has disturbed Pauline. The Gilley family—and the college itself—are *unholy communities* in which legalism has replaced respect. The only way to correct such inadequacies, Levin believes, is through constant struggle.

Of course, the tone is mock-heroic, but the son becomes a father—a hero of sorts. First he rebels by proclaiming his interest in the chairmanship, opposing Gilley; he wants, in other words, to rule. He is unsuccessful—outsmarted by the father. But he triumphs (over the law?) when he takes Pauline and the children with him—his new life is the new family. His victory is slightly hollow because he cannot teach anywhere—the academic world is not his spiritual domain. Levin, the father, must teach at home. Can these lessons be enough? Malamud thinks so.

Philip Roth's sense of family is strong. Eli Peck is another uncertain son who finds his spiritual father in Tzuref, the principal. During their first conversation (or lesson) "half-dying shouts of children at play" roll in through the window. Tzuref is the guardian of children; Eli cannot tolerate their "mysterious babble." The lawyer, in effect wants to destroy them by removing their residence from Woodenton. Later we see him at home, soothed and protected by his wife—as Tzuref protects his children. This protection helps to incapacitate him: Eli is a sick child for his "psychologist"—wife—and for the community fathers who command him to do his job properly.

The son wants to flee from the father—as Shapiro runs from Messias—because the old man incarnates Jewish tradition. Tzuref frightens him, threatening to unbalance his safe, sacrilegious existence. But Eli draws closer to him; this attraction increases as the lawyer's own child waits to be born. Roth symbolically relates the new child to the new Eli. And in several strange scenes his hero, in effect, gasps for air, pushes, and screams while he is reborn. The story—the transformation itself—grows in intensity until Eli, after his revelation of the Jewish Experience which transcends generations, runs to the hospital wanting to see his son. Miraculously he has understood, that like Tzuref, he must care for the young. He is now the father. "But he rose, suddenly, as though up out of a dream, and flailing his arms, screamed: *'I'm the father!'*"

Letting Go has for one epigraph Wallace Stevens'

lines: "The son / And the father alike and equally are spent." It is a novel of fathers and sons; it accurately captures the fragmentation of the Jewish-American family.

Gabe Wallach is a young man who always gets into "entangling alliances." He must, in effect, "help" others; he is another "mad crusader" who, like Eli, offers himself—indeed, sacrifices himself—without knowing why. He agrees to help Paul and Libby Herz adopt a child (of a presumably unwed mother). Of course, his assistance is messy. The plot becomes slightly melodramatic—blackmail, violent threats—but the important thing is that Gabe loses money and gains knowledge: *it is better not to impose oneself upon others; benevolence can be destructive. Let go.* Gabe's transformation, unlike Eli's, is neither complete nor convincing—although he recognizes that his sloppy benevolence is guilt-ridden and guileless, he lets go easily, almost coolly.

The adoption reinforces the idea of family in the entire novel. Gabe says: "I was of course racing back to familiar problems of my own." Because his mother insists in her last letter that she has always "pulled" at people, and his father constantly calls him long-distance, he has never been able to free himself of an irresponsible lust for "benevolence." He has remained confused about proper values. Roth gives us many related ironies. Mr. Wallach, a dentist, loves to take care of his son's teeth; he must have him home for holidays. He senses, however, that this excess love is wrong. Later Mr. Wallach marries again—another adoption! —because he can't stand alone. Obviously, Gabe, like his father, is unsure about his role—son or father? Even when he lets go, he appears to follow his father's footsteps: he is "hooked."

Now the father-son relationship is funny and bitter—like Fiedler's. But Roth widens his view; he shows another family struggle. Paul Herz has alienated himself from his parents by marrying a Gentile. They command him—for his own benefit?—to leave. Carrying "the rock of his heart," he returns in time to see his father's funeral. Suddenly he accepts actuality: "For his truth was revealed to him, his final premise melted away." Despite his former belief in his own "greatness," Paul is, after all, a son—even more, an orphan. It is too fitting that he adopts—with Gabe's help—a child.

Paul and Gabe lack correct principles (even though Paul "accepts" his father). They join the other sons in Jewish-American literature who cannot live in the world of their fathers or their own world. They dangle without the patriarchal "sainthood" of Tzuref or Morris Bober.

4   TIME

ABRAHAM JOSHUA HESCHEL has written that "Judaism is *a religion of history, a religion of time*. The God of Israel was not found primarily in the facts of nature. He spoke through events in history. While the deities of other peoples were associated with places or things, the God of the prophets was the God of events: the Redeemer from slavery, the Revealer of the Torah, manifesting Himself in events of history rather than in things or places." [1] Because Judaism is history-intoxicated, it is different from those religions which stress contempt for time and love of eternity—from those religions which stress contempt for time and Hindu and Greek religion. But it does not assume that time is always the same—it believes, as Heschel indicates, that "there is a hierarchy of moments within time, that all ages are not alike." [2] Judaism is loyal to sacred moments. Thus recollection becomes a guiding principle: current events are measured in relation to chosen moments. Arthur Hertzberg tells us that "God's initial covenant, with Abraham, was with the head of a family, and the Jewish people was conceived as the ever-increasing number of his descendants. Hence to this day the convert to Judaism is not only accepted into the faith; the ritual prescribes that he be adopted into the family as a child of Abraham." [3] The Jew

believes in the God who revealed Himself to the patriarchs.

Contrast him to the archetypal American. He has
no deep sense of history, going back when the patri-
otic occasion demands, only to the Founding Fathers
and the Constitution. American history is *new*. This
newness has always been appealing for exiles from old
lands. Crèvecoeur writes in 1782 that the traveler to
America has "arrived on a new continent; a modern
society offers itself to his contemplation, different from
what he had hitherto seen." De Tocqueville in 1840
writes that "in America, society seems to live from
hand to mouth, like an army in the field. Nevertheless,
the art of administration is undoubtedly a science, and
no sciences can be improved if the discoveries and observations of successive generations are not connected
together in the order in which they occur." R. W. B.
Lewis, in describing Whitman's fascination with the
new, writes that *Leaves of Grass* is a "Yankee Genesis:
a new account of the creation of the world—the
creation that is of a new world; an account this time
with a happy ending for Adam its hero; or better yet,
with no ending at all; and with this important emen-
dation, that now the creature has taken on the role of
creator." [4]

Of course, the Jewish and American views can lead
to distortions. The American can become so obsessed
with newness that he forgets the power of the past.
When he does, he is haunted by a sense of something
missing. R. W. B. Lewis describes Hawthorne's "return into time." There are many Gothic tales which
present—as do Hawthorne's—the spiritual ugliness of
the man without history: "Rip Van Winkle,"
"Bartleby, the Scrivener," and "The Jolly Corner"—
to name only a few. Newness—or "Adamic thinking"—can, ironically, lead to obsession with the past. [5]

But Jewish concern only for the past can lead to present maladjustment. The Jew lives in the modern world; can he keep his rituals despite the onslaughts of screaming telephones, different Sabbaths, and substitute faiths? Can he believe in *evolution?* The Jew, it seems, must confront the present, aware that he has fared better (and will fare better) *once upon a time*. To quote Will Herberg: "We need not deny that there has been notable progress made in various fields of human life and in various periods of human history, or that we always stand under the obligation to enhance human welfare on all fronts. But we must challenge any doctrine that transforms progress into a cosmic force capable of redeeming mankind and completing the meaning of history." [6]

We cannot really separate time from exile and family life. The three themes are bound inextricably. The son views his father as the incarnation of the past; his exile from traditional authority—from the Promised Land which *was* or *may be*—is his *present* condition: it is all he really knows. Our writers deal with the time-dimension (as theme and structure) because they are divided. Do they respond as Jews or Americans to the past? Is their response odd?

In many of his poems Karl Shapiro precisely captures present phenomena—the drug store, the emporium, the Buick. But he does not seem to be comfortable in satirizing "mechanized" values. He turns to the past in his *Poems of a Jew*, and contrasts the honorable past to the dishonorable present.

"The Alphabet" uses the Hebrew language as a symbol of living tradition. The "letters of the Jews," Shapiro writes, lean through "perfect ages"; they sing through "solid stone." These letters represent the power to resist and survive each historical period—like the synagogue they embody "patient time" (or eternity?). The Jew lives in his letters—therefore, when

Shapiro looks at them he remembers—as do the psalmists—the uniqueness of history. He remembers the "tipsy idols of the Roman," the fires of the ghettos and in this ritualistic act, he relives, as it were, the past of his ancestors. The present is transcended, if only briefly. Shapiro ends his poem with the vision of judgment day when the "book of days" completely reveals the meaning of time.

"The Olive Tree" is similar. Shapiro gazes at this tree, recognizing that it is filled with holy attributes. It reminds him of the biblical past. He must reclaim his heritage (if only the capacity of endurance) and he sheds his tennis shoes to walk on the fallen olives "in love and reverence." Tennis shoes and "ancient" olives—in this contradiction (or transcendence?) lies the meaning of history. Contrast this act with the last stanza of "The Phenomenon." Here Shapiro warns us against the forgetfulness of history: "But one day all was clear, and one day soon, / Sooner than those who witnessed it had died, / Nature herself forgot the phenomenon, / Her faulty snowfall brilliantly denied." The black snowfall—a symbol of Fascism—must be remembered even when Nature later corrects itself. In such remembrance lies the ability of men to live fully.

No wonder that in his critical book, *In Defense of Ignorance*, Shapiro attacks Eliot, Yeats, and Pound—the "trinity" of Modern Poetry as he calls them—for neglecting history. The three poets cannot tolerate modern life; they flee from it into a never-never land called Tradition: they "adulate the Tradition, accepting the "fall" of man from Civilization, and an esthetic Ideal which is capable of reinstating the artist as the carrier of Civilization." But their Tradition is only a false system based on a misreading—or complete disregard—of the way things really were. They worship an Ideal Past. Shapiro is especially harsh toward

The Waste Land—its "mythic" style is "worthless and not even true"—because it symbolizes the whole tendency of Modern Poetry to corrupt fact, to accept partial historical truths. As a Jew he realizes that the past carries ideal *and* real meaning and that, consequently, it cannot be glamorized to serve an escapist purpose.

In contrast to Eliot, Shapiro refuses to forget the historical *lapses* of the Jews or his own. His faithful memory is evident in "Shylock" and "Recapitulations." The first—like "The Murder of Moses"—is a recreation of the past. Shylock is not viewed as a completely wronged man; on the contrary, he displays unconcealed hatred which arises partially from his inability to look at past or future: he is "incurious / As to the future, totally clear of blame." He lives in the present, taking care of his ledgers—unaware of the forces which have made him this way. He resembles the amputee of "The Leg" who lives in "the middle distance"—a "twilight-sleep." When Shapiro writes the autobiographical "Recapitulations," he is equally brutal toward himself. "Mornings I practiced piano, / Wrote elegies and sighed; / The evenings were conversations / Of poetry and suicide." These brief autobiographies demonstrate that he must start at the beginning, to go beyond accurate presentation of cars and drugstores to understand his stance in the world. They "present the evidence as I see it, the states of mind which in my case led to the writing of poems." Poetry, Shapiro implies, realistically scrutinizes the past.

Delmore Schwartz' "work is for the most part turned toward the past, toward his own past." [7] The early poems deal with time, "the school in which we learn."

"The Ballad of the Children of the Czar" is typical.

The narrator juxtaposes his own past in Brooklyn when "Franklin D. Roosevelt / Was an Arrow Collar ad" to earlier events on the world scene. He pictures the Czar's children playing ball—they are innocent without history. They do not belong, as it were, to time. Neither does the narrator at the age of two— he calls himself "irrational." But at the very time that children are free, events occuring without their knowledge will influence them. Thus while the narrator eats a baked potato, his grandfather "coughs" in the Russian army. History is terrifying because it forms the individual without his knowledge, and he must spend his mature years reliving it—not only his but his father's. Now we can see the reason for the bouncing ball of the Czar's children. *Time, in effect, is that ball.* It eludes our hands; it is too big for us; it is " a pitiless, purposeless thing."

"Calmly We Walk through This April's Day" echoes the ballad. Again we have a narrator who lives in the present, walking calmly this April's day in 1937. But his outing is disturbed by thoughts of past and future. He wonders "what will become of you and me" besides "the photo and the memory." Alternating with these thoughts of the future is the knowledge that time is the fire in which we burn." How can the self survive in such a blaze? The narrator considers himself a child "ravished entirely in . . . passing play." As the poem progresses, his questioning increases: Where is his father? Where is his sister? Where is 1914 to the present? There are no answers to such inevitable, necessary questions—only flashes of pain and the hope that memory can triumph over time.

"Time's Dedication" begins with many present participles: "My heart beating, my blood running." These participles present activity, motion, lack of calm—

they bounce like the ball of the Czar's children. The clock is "quick-ticking"—and the short syllables intensify the speed. Present time "dies perpetually." The narrator cries Halt! Stand still! But his commands to blood and beauty do not help—they die in (or with) time. Only love—in this poem it supplants memory as a weapon against the enemy—has the possibility of stopping time. The narrator slows his rhythm—deliberately, deliberately. But the slowness is less effective, less personal, than the preceding turmoil.

Schwartz' exile from the past (and his involvement in it) is repeated in his stories, especially in those dealing with family life.

"In Dreams Begin Responsibilities" begins with the sentence, "I think it is the year 1909." The ambiguity of time is immediately established: although we live in it, we cannot really understand it; we don't know how to measure it. Time is likened to a silent movie—it has sudden flashes, "dots and rays."

The narrator looks at the motion picture of the past; he sees his father walk down the Brooklyn streets to visit his fiancée. They meet; they court each other. But just as the scene is to be completed—just as the narrator can *see* the past—the film breaks! Then it is fixed, only to repeat itself before continuing the scene. During the scene the narrator weeps, realizing that he cannot scream to the actors, to the past, to perform in a different way, to exist more perfectly. The past is comical and sad. The film goes on; the courtship is played out—and the narrator cries again when he sees the "terrifying sun and the terrifying ocean." (Remember "Far Rockaway.") He leaves his seat and goes to the men's room, returning to find that he has again missed part of the film.

New images crowd the screen. There are his parents on the "merry-go-round." The merry-go-round, like the bouncing ball, represents the whirling force of time—not only can't the narrator bridge the gap to the past—his parents (all people) cannot control their present movements. How to help them? How to help himself? The narrator screams at the film: Don't marry! He does not want to be born. But the film continues and while his parents have their pictures taken and, later, have their fortunes read, the narrator becomes more and more agitated until he views himself "walking a tight-rope a hundred feet over a circus-audience and suddenly the rope is showing signs of breaking, and I get up from my seat and begin to shout once more the first words I can think of to communicate my terrible fear." And he wakes up from his long dream to find that he is twenty-one. Can he master the unique past which has formed his present anxiety?

The weight of the past, the "bouncing" of the present—both are clear in "A Bitter Farce." Shenandoah Fish teaches Navy students during World War II. He emphasizes "elementary things." However, they ask him embarrassing questions about his "liberalism." Shenandoah is constricted; "his inner being [is] suddenly full of fear and trembling . . ." because he cannot answer them. He flees. But in his other classes he is confronted by other pressing questions. Miss Eberhart writes a paper about the demanding, grasping, "almost unscrupulous" Jews. Shenandoah still controls his feelings, discussing her bias in a methodical, correct manner. When he once more meets his Navy students, the Jewish Question arises again and he can no longer control himself. He uses logic to battle anti-semitism—this fails. He uses compassion—this fails. Then he confesses his Jewishness: "I feel very proud of my ancestors." The story makes a stronger point. Shenandoah gives up his chance to report Murphy for his lack of discretion, his anti-

semitic remarks, because of "events which had occurred for the past five thousand years." The personal
past of the previous story is expanded here into the
Jewish Past, but both Schwartz' heroes dangle in
time.

The verse play, *Shenandoah*, begins with the narrator, Shenandoah, waiting to look at the center of the
stage, where he will see his past—his name-giving. He
is separated from that past while he is in it. This
paradox informs the entire play. Shenandoah says
"stand at my point of view, / Regard with my emotion
the small event / Which gave my mind and gave my
character, / Amid the hundred thousand possibilities
/ Heredity and community avail, / Bound and engender, the very life I know!" Again Schwartz uses the
device of a "screen"—a "play within the play." As the
curtain rises, Shenandoah gazes at the "moment of
time, seen in its pastness": he sees the period furniture, the busyness of his mother. He thinks of Aris-
totle's union of "particular and universal," and his
philosophical remarks not only interpret his relation
to his heritage but also record his estrangement from
it. The play abounds in irony which tries to maintain
balance but slips into sadness. When Shenandoah
regards his parents' marriage, he knows it "is a stupid
endless mistake"—one which has made him into a
sensitive, disturbed person. But he cannot control the
past event; it controls him. He can only carry it with
humility.

What causes his parents to give him his odd name?
Is it Europe? Is it America? Is it the fear of death? Is it
the desire of the lower middle class to "imitate the sick
elite"? There is not one answer. The past event—or
trauma—is created by "world-wide causes." Shenandoah cries, "Poor child, the center of this sinful earth,
/ How many world-wide powers surround you." The

43840

"child is the meaning of this life"—to quote a Schwartz title.

This insistence upon the uniqueness of personal and racial history is clear in Isaac Rosenfeld's fiction. Like Schwartz, he tends to use a narrator who recollects an event which has assumed such extraordinary significance that it becomes "sacred."

Passage from Home begins with the words "I remember the year"; it examines that crucial series of events in which, as we have already seen, Bernard matures quickly. There are several interesting "uses of the past" in the novel. Bernard pictures the Passover Seder in which the Jews remember their ancestors' flight from Egypt. The Seder is different from all other meals of the year; it is drenched in time: a bit tipsy, he sees "the original Egypt, colored and revived, the parting of the waters, the Red Sea agape, the journey through the desert." The uniqueness of Jewish history counterpoints the burden of personal history. Because Aunt Minna had *once* fled from the family she cannot return; because the father had run away, he cannot properly face his son—such events color the present, compelling Bernard to realize that he cannot reform the world—let along create a Utopian future—until he grasps the meaning of the past. He returns to an earlier vision of memory.

> Memory resembles the old photographs lying about the house, pasted in albums, buried in drawers, pictures which begged to be believed, showing my father as a young man, my mother as a girl, myself as a baby. These images were too oblique a version of the familiar, too greatly altered, completely negated in life. I would sometimes stare at the snapshot of my father, my eyes fixed to the softer and younger face, each line and hair of it, hoping I might thereby gain some understanding, a clue, perhaps still available in the past,

to undo that in the present which was entirely a secret. But even the younger face denied me; I would stare until my eyes teared over and the image began to dissolve. So with my own snapshot, a baby, ball in hand, seated on a rug. This being I might never again enter.

The narrator of "Coney Island Revisited," like Bernard, is estranged from the past he must master. He tells us that "it was not until the other day, when I returned on a visit to Coney Island, that I recalled an important episode of my youth which had been buried all these years." The recollection made him think how "far back" he had started. Eighteen years ago he worked in the sideshow, mixing T. S. Eliot with his spiel; he was contemptuous of the other workers and the dopey audience. He sneered at the world. He was like the "mechanical dummy"—a grotesque object removed from humanity. Only when he began to desire stupid Gladys, another worker, did he realize his "mechanization." He taunted her; he played with her feelings. Finally the two clashed in desire. They tried to "go the limit" in the funhouse, but he could not satisfy her. Now as he walks away from the sideshow, he is "shocked to think I should ever have been capable of doing such things; but in the intervening years, how much had I altered?" He cannot reply to his question: his eyes reach "for the silence of the ocean."

Joseph Feigenbaum in "The Hand That Fed Me" is also haunted. He writes to Ellen, a Gentile girl, trying to explain his complex feelings toward her. He *once* met her! The meeting, however, assumed such symbolic value that he cannot rest until he understands the entire incident. His awkward philosophical letters are filled with notions about time. On December 29 he writes, "And so, if I go out of my way and out of my time to reach after a promised happiness of three years back, this, too, a deliberate delusion, is also at my expense." The past has become glorious because he is presently unhappy; he has invented an Ideal Past to relieve him of anxiety. But while he worships a girl he cannot embrace—and a time which never existed, except in his own mind—he knows that such pure vision, such escape into non-existence, is dangerous. On December 31 he writes, "And if a man will attach, as I have done, a whole morality to a single incident, he will always be at the mercy of 'incidents.' The insight he will gain will give him no peace." He is thus another dangling man—removed from past (by screening it falsely) and from present. We wonder whether the New Year will find him really "different."

"Negro and Jew: Encounter in America" is a characteristic essay by Leslie Fiedler. Although it begins as a review of *Notes of a Native Son*, it is primarily concerned with time. Fiedler takes us back to the beginning; he assumes that the Negro and the Jew accept roles which "they have played no part in creating." The Jew, he tells us, is a late-comer to America; when he arrives, "he and America are already set in their respective ways." The Jew carries the burden of ancient history, "the memory of a world he cannot afford to and does not want to deny." The Negro, however, arrives in America without a past, but he soon assumes a central role in its history. Because he is tossed into historical consciousness he feels uneasy, making the white man feel the same way. But Fiedler does not stop here. The Negro and the Jew exist "in the timeless limbo of the psyche." Although we can date their arrivals in America we cannot ever know when they first assumed certain symbolic burdens. The important thing is this: Negro and Jew—whatever their *actual* past—have a "timeless" past created by the white Christian mind. *Both not only have to contend with events which really happened to them (or their ancestors) but with events which are attributed to them.* Thus they are obsessed with the nature of time.

And Fiedler turns to his own past. He cannot speculate about such abstractions without confronting those events which have made him deal with time—and two minorities' involvement in it. At the age of thirteen he was friends with a "colored porter." Despite his closeness to this man—they shared their lunches—he could not accept him as "a person" but as "a type." This early insight into the differences between person and type—between *real* past and *imagined* past—is not to leave him. Fiedler remembers other events—walking to school in the Negro neighborhood, selling shoes to Negro customers. Memories flood his mind. Finally he thinks that he as Jew resembles the Negro, except that he is shadowed by the special knowledge that "No Jew can selflessly dedicate himself to the fight for the equality of the Negro; when he pretends that he is not also fighting for himself, he is pretending that he is indistinguishable from a *goy*." Because he has confronted the complexity of personal and racial time, he is more "emancipated" than an innocent Feigenbaum.

In a section of *No! in Thunder* entitled "The Generations" Fiedler deals with time as burden (and glory?). His first essay is, superfically, a review of a scholarly book, *The Twenties*, by F. J. Hoffman, but it is really an attack on the "statistical" past. History, he seems to be saying, cannot be charted simply or scientifically; it is more than numbers. "When [Hoffman] is not being victimized by the notion that the 'actual past' resides in newspaper files, he quite realizes the subtlety of the relationship he sets out to describe; and he is admirably on guard against certain standard oversimplifications." But Hoffman does believe, nevertheless, that the truth "is in the verifiable, the statistical 'fact.'" Fiedler opposes D. H. Lawrence to Hoffman because Lawrence believes in the "resurrected past" rather than the "reconstructed past." He, of course, is for Lawrence—as we have seen by his use of the resurrected past in "Negro and Jew."

When we consider "Roman Holiday," we note that Fiedler's concern with time is again linked to the Jews. The first paragraph contrasts the crazy present to the wise past—the confused tourists to the disciples—and the contrasts continue. Rome is presented as the "eternal city" which contains the burdens of the Jewish Past—the Arch of Titus, the "Corso where the *ebrei* were once forced to race against asses," the Tiber which holds the Temple's Golden Candlestick. In this history-drenched city, modern Jews are "alien." In the ghetto the Parker 51 replaces the Candlestick. There are, indeed, two different Seders—for younger men and older men. Thus Fiedler is thrown out of time; wanting to resurrect the past, he must combat those without history. And this conflict between generations is inevitable. In "The Un-Angry Young Men," a later essay, Fiedler contrasts his past—"first violence and despair, the flirtation with failure and the commitment to radical politics; then all savor of slow disenchantment; and only at long last the acceptance of responsibility and accommodation"—to the Adamic thinking of the post-war generation. Our youth, he says, live in a state of dullness because they are without a past; their ideals are simply the clichés of previous generations. Curiously, they are *old*, not having tested their violence or wildness—their youth.

All these ideas are dramatized (even more strongly)

in *The Second Stone*. Time is at the heart of this novel. We first see Hilda and Clem as displaced persons in Rome. They do not know how to respond to History; they joke about it. Clem says, "What are you doing in Rome anyhow, Hilda? And why am I playing the clown beside you in this underground tourist trap?" Because they live in the "loony" twentieth-century—an age so "new" that it seems not to belong to time—they cannot handle the past with respect or reverence. Yet they realize—especially Clem—that they oddly reflect precious generations of Americans—the innocents abroad. They live a historical role without complete understanding or acceptance. (They resemble Negro and Jew in America.) Only after they admit the influence of such historical role-playing, can they differentiate themselves from, say, Mark Twain's characters.

But they have another problem. They are removed, by ignorance, from their *personal* past. Hilda tells us much later that she married Mark because of a poem he once wrote. When Clem informs her that his name is really Mark (or Marcus), that *he* wrote the poem, she is overwhelmed. Her whole life has been built on a faulty premise. Can she give birth not only to the child she carries in her womb but to a new self? Can Clem reclaim his past identity? Fiedler deliberately puns. He does more: he upsets stereotypes—the Good Mother; the Wise Rabbi; the Gentile; the Jew—to make us see the comedy which arises from immature timelessness. His adults are children wearing masks. When they acknowledge the inevitable power of the past, they can understand the age in which they are thrown. Then their rituals will be true, not simply grotesque parodies of ancient ones (as in the Last Supper which ends the novel).

Time plays an important part in Saul Bellow's

fiction, especially in *The Victim* and *Seize the Day*.

In *The Victim* Allbee and Asa lack any whole view of time. They see the past, the present, or the future in one-sided, discontinuous ways. They break "connections"—as the phone connection on the first page is broken or the bell of Elena's house is disconnected.

The past is the one aspect of time respected—and feared—by the "victims." Allbee is haunted by his lost job, claiming that he was fired because of Asa's "crazy" replies to Rudiger. This past event has assumed overwhelming importance, destroying the future for him. The "original sin," which he cannot understand or accept, confronts Asa. He discovers dark meanings in the past, disregarding the present and the future. He begins to be haunted by the "curse" of the past. First he remembers the interview with Rudiger, then his dead mother. The fears of madness—is it *inherited?*— pressure him.

Bellow relates this fear of the past to a deterministic philosophy. Allbee thrusts the philosophy at Asa. "You don't agree that people have a destiny forced on them? Well, that's ridiculous, because they do. And that's all the destiny they get, so they'd better not assume they're running their own show." He constantly repeats the idea of destiny, compelling Asa to think "there was a wrong, a general wrong." Both see currents drowning them—drowning everyone.

One of Asa's dreams emphasizes horrifying determinism. He finds himself in a train station, carrying a heavy suitcase, pushing through the crowd. Although he has missed the train—the past "overshadows" the present!—he has another chance to board the train because a "second section of it" is due to leave in three minutes. Asa can still change things, impose order. But when he tries to enter through a certain gate, two men tell him: This gate isn't open to the

public; "You can't go back the way you came, either."
Asa is pushed into the alley; his face is covered with
tears. It seems that "missing the train" is irrevocable.

Asa sees the split between generations; at least he is
moving towards an understanding of change. But he
sees change as erratic or violent. He thinks of his
father once saying how many foreign children, Italian
or Irish, died. How strange, Asa thinks, if his father
"could know that his own grandson was one of these,
buried in a Catholic cemetery." The last scene suggests that the problem of time remains. Asa sees
Allbee no longer depressed, poor, mad. He engages
him in a metaphoric conversation about the train.
Allbee claims that he is the type that "comes to terms
with whoever runs things." He hasn't missed the train;
he has adjusted to its scheduled movement. Asa asks,
"what's your idea of who runs things?" There is no
reply. Bellow suggests that we must accept the past as
controlling us—but we should come to terms with it
by seizing the day. Only this act recovers our freedom.

Time plays an important part in *Seize the Day* (as is
obvious from the title). Tommy Wilhelm is, at first, a
non-believer in myth or ritual—the eternal return. He
thinks of the past as obsessively as do Asa and Allbee.
He *was once* successful: he *made* a decent living; he
was happily married; he *was* close to his father. Because he defines himself in relation to a "wonderful
past," he has no real future. Like the old men and
women in the hotel, he has "nothing to do but wait
out the day." Of course, I have simplified the conception. Tommy does have a "future" in the speculation
schemes of Dr. Tamkin. Money, success, self-
realization—all these wait for him in the stock exchange. But time is not seized by the hero; it is fragmented and idealized. Time is actually a *hole* for him.

Dr. Tamkin offers a solution. "The spiritual compensation is what I look for. Bringing people into the here-and-now. The real universe. That's the present moment. The past is no good to us. The future is full of anxiety." Although this solution appears to be vital, it is different from a whole view of time—the one found in Augie's concern with Einhorn as Croesus. Tamkin is also breaking time: the present becomes all-important—which is as bad as Tommy's "backward" vision. We should seize the day, but we should see it as linking all days, as part of a never-ending cycle.

The end of *Seize the Day* suggests that Tommy discovers the "eternal return." After his loss on the stock exchange, he wanders into a funeral parlor. Here it is "dark and cool"—time is forgotten. Only the terrible fact of the human condition is present. Tommy is "past words, past reason, coherence"—past entrapment by time. He has a vision of *all* men in the coffin and when he sobs incessantly, he is cleansed of his problems. He suffers ecstasy.

"The Loan" demonstrates Bernard Malamud's concern with time. We are immediately introduced to the "heady smell of Lieb's white bread"—to the successful present. But as soon as we are placed in this time, we meet Kobotsky, an "old friend" of Lieb, who enters to disturb things. He stresses that he is from "long ago." Lieb can talk about old times. "The world was new. We were, Kobotsky, young. Do you remember how both together, immigrants out of steerage, we registered in night school?" Such nostalgia is easy. But when Kobotsky requests a loan, Lieb is shaken and although he agrees—after all, he *once* borrowed from his friend—he finally submits to furious Bessie, his wife. He is in the middle: the past and present have different claims on him. The best Lieb can do is mourn youth. "Kobotsky and the baker embraced and

sighed over their lost youth. They pressed mouths
together and parted forever."

Time is always a burden to Malamud's heroes. They
are unhappy because they constantly remember the
past (which may or may not have been happy). They
find it difficult to adjust, to change, although they
know they must. They care little about the future—
they find the present unbearable enough. They see
fragments of time which they cannot connect.

Let us look closely at *The Assistant*. The first page
introduces Morris' relation to time. He lives "compul-
sively," getting up early each morning to sell a roll to
the Polish woman. The present "rings" constantly. Or
it moves slowly, dully. Morris is trapped in time.
"When times were bad time was bad. It died as he
waited, stinking in his nose." He cannot really wait
and he cannot stop waiting. He views time as the
enemy. Thus he tries to retreat from such struggle—
"he wishes fleetingly that he could once more be out in
the open, as when he was a boy." He idealizes the past,
but when the meat provisions man enters, he is shut-
tled back to the monotonous, deadly present. The
details mount; they drown Morris as time entombs
him. His wife and daughter also harp on the past—to
the exclusion of anything else. Ida, the wife, remembers the old Jewish neighborhood; Helen remembers
(more unhappily) the loss of her virginity. Both have
no future—let alone present. Only outsiders think of
such things: Karp's son, the meat provisions man. The
Bobers have lost touch with the wheel of time.

> "Why did you let me sleep so long?" the grocer com-
> plained.
> [Ida] didn't answer.
> "Yesterday or today's paper?"
> "Yesterday."

Later Frank Alpine joins them. The past also haunts him. He must reclaim it; he must *atone* for it. He tells Morris, "Sometimes I think your life keeps going the way it starts out on you." Because Frank is "determined," he can sympathize with these Jews who, in effect, have been chosen—a long time ago—to bear a historic burden. But he and Morris must carry the burden with strength and joy. They must, in other words, start living now. This is why Malamud emphasizes "possibilities." Possibilities, for them, should exist in the present. When they see clearly what they are doing now, they can be reborn: they can seize the day.

After Frank begins to work in the store, there are more exciting details—more exciting *moments*. Time is filled with active, meaningful life. Frank courts Helen; he cleans the store; customers come more often and stay longer. Yet the past continues to exert influence—and rightly so; eventually it will have to be repaid, if not conquered. Frank muses, "This thought had lived in him with claws; or like a thirst he could never spit out, a repulsive need to get out of his system all that had happened . . . ; to change the beginning, beginning with the past that always stupendously stank up the now—to change his life before the smell of it suffocated him." How do Malamud's exiles repay the past? How do they *reopen* time? They extend themselves by loving one another. When Helen thinks of Frank's desire for knowledge, she faces the future (if only as a daydream). "The future offered more in the way of realizable possibilities, Helen thought, if a person dared take a chance with it." Frank resists Ward Minogue—the urge to repeat the criminal, sinful past. Yet the past, history, still claims them. Malamud does not allow them ever to escape it, but he suggests in the last chapters that they can accept that burden and live with it. After Frank "becomes" Morris, even getting up early for the Polish woman, he transcends his own past. He adopts, as it were, the "eternal present" of Morris' daily routine. He does more: he carries on this present, lengthening it into the future. He extends time—it is now a gift for Helen (and himself). Thus *The Assistant* ends like *Seize the Day*: the wheel of time asserts itself; in its painful, ecstatic motion lies all events.

In contrast to Malamud's past-dominated Jews, Philip Roth's Jews are youthful and "streamlined." They embrace the American myth, trying to forget the European or immigrant past. They dangle in the present.

"Goodbye, Columbus" can be read in this way. Neil Klugman tells us that his orthodox Aunt Gladys is out of time; she still believes in the "Poor Jews in Palestine." Her old-world view is "crazy" because it does not acknowledge those New Jews, like the Patimkins, who belong to country clubs. But Neil is rather harsh. These New Jews, he sees later, are just as disoriented. Their "heaven"—he emphasizes ironically heaven, the afterlife, and eternity in the first few pages—is also silly. They live without their Newark past. (Newark and Short Hills stand, rather conveniently, for the past and the present. Only the traveler between them can cope with real time.) But the Patimkins cannot really deny their previous existence. Although they may hide their "tall old refrigerator—its ancient presence was a reminder of the Patimkin roots in Newark"—it is still in their house. Mr. Patimkin works in an old Newark neighborhood (in which he feels comfortable), and he cannot really leave it. These New Jews, unsure about time, seek to transcend it or, better yet, to trick it. They resemble the mothers Neil sees: "they looked immortal sitting there." Their immortality is grotesque.

Although Neil hates such immortality, he believes that he can find nothing in Jewish history to sustain him. He is left without any awareness of sacred moments. Aunt Gladys cannot help him. Mr. Patimkin cannot help him. Perhaps Leo, Brenda's uncle, can point the way: at least he sees something of value in the past, but he is also trapped by progress—the deliberate negation of history. His light bulbs compete against the new ones; their *quality* loses. It is appropriate, therefore, that Neil ends his goodbye to the Old and New Jews by violating Jewish tradition: he does not celebrate the New Year. But is this solution more than an empty rebellious gesture?

Contrast him to "Epstein." Although *he* is removed from the present—unable to understand the crazy youth around him—he does acknowledge the power of the past. He is "historical." He mourns the death of his son many years before, the loss of his own youth, and the business he had built "from the ground." These memories disturb him but, strangely, they make him more alive—more Jewish—than the grotesque mothers in "Goodbye, Columbus." Roth thus gives us another displaced person, desperately trying to adjust to time, and losing. But Epstein's struggle is more heroic than Neil's simple, "timeless" rebellion.

Ozzie, Eli, Epstein, and Neil—they are on the edge, attracted to and repelled by the Jewish Past. Their plight is perhaps more extreme and futile than that of Shenandoah Fish, Bernard, or Tommy Wilhelm, but they join these other heroes. They lack their ancestors' confidence in sacred events, in the uniqueness of history.

JEWISH TRADITION contains many tensions.

> Jewish thinking and living can only be adequately understood in terms of a dialectical pattern, containing opposite or contrasted properties. As in a magnet, the ends of which have opposite magnetic qualities, these terms are opposite to one another and exemplify a *polarity* which lies at the very heart of Judaism, the polarity of ideas and events, of mitsvah and sin, of kavanah and deed, of regularity and spontaneity, of uniformity and individuality, of halacha and agada, of law and inwardness, of love and fear, of understanding and obedience, of joy and discipline, of the good and the evil drive, of time and eternity.[1]

But perhaps the most significant tension is that of intellect and feeling, head and heart.

Jewish respect for learning is, of course, quite evident throughout history. Judah ibn Tibbon captures it poetically in a testament addressed to his son.

> My son! Make your books your companions, let your cases and shelves be your pleasure grounds and gardens. Bask in their paradise, gather their fruit, pluck their roses, take their spices and their myrrh. If your soul be satiate and weary, change from garden to garden, from furrow to furrow, from prospect to prospect.[2]

The Talmud tells us: "Our masters taught: / A sage takes precedence over a king of Israel; / if a sage dies, we have none like him— / if a king dies, all Israel are eligible for kingship." [3] However, along with the respect for books, is the fear that constant intellectualization is "usleless" or dangerous. Several Yiddish proverbs express this antagonism: "The less a man understands, the better off he is." [4] "As you are at seven, so you are at seventy." [5] "Reason is a slow-poke." [6] Israel Baal Shem agrees.

> The end-all of knowledge is to know that we cannot know anything. But there are two sorts of not-knowing. The one is the immediate not-knowing, when a man does not even begin to examine and try to know, because it is impossible to know. Another, however, examines and seeks, until he comes to know that one cannot know. [7]

Jewish tradition turns to feeling which cures "rationalism." Abraham Joshua Heschel writes, "Reverence, love, prayer, faith go beyond the acts of shallow reasoning." [8] "For all the appreciation of reason and our thankfulness for it, man's intelligence was never regarded in Jewish tradition as being self-sufficient. 'Trust in the Lord with all thy heart, and do not rely on thine own understanding' (Proverbs 3:5)" [9] One Hasidic master puts it succinctly. "The chief source of understanding lies in the heart." [10] We should not assume that feeling must triumph over intellect; there should be a wedding of the two.

> The employment of reason is indispensable to the understanding and worship of God, and religion withers without it. The insights of faith are general, vague, and stand in need of conceptualization in order to be communicated to the mind, integrated and brought to consistency. Without reason faith becomes blind. With-

out reason we would not know how to apply the insights of faith to the concrete issues of living.[11]

Classic American literature gives us the same tensions. Head fights heart. Hawthorne, and James—to name only two—deal with the hero who intellectualizes to such a great extent that he forgets his feelings—his humanity. They affirm the curative power of compassion.

Hawthorne describes Hollingsworth's rationalism in *The Blithedale Romance*.

He was not altogether human. There was something else in Hollingsworth besides flesh and blood, and sympathies and affections and celestial spirit.

This is always true of those men who have surrendered themselves to an overwhelming purpose. It does not so much impel them from without, nor even operate as a motive power within, but grows incorporate with all that they think and feel, and finally converts them into little else save that one principle. When such begins to be the predicament, it is not cowardice, but wisdom to avoid these victims. They have no heart, no sympathy, no reason, no conscience. They will keep no friend, unless he make himself the mirror of their purpose; they will smite and slay you, and trample your dead corpse under foot, all the more readily, if you take the first step with them, and cannot take the second, and the third, and every other step of their terribly strait path. They have an idol to which they consecrate themselves high-priest, and deem it holy work to offer sacrifices of whatever is most precious; and never once seem to suspect—so cunning has the Devil been with them—that this false deity, in whose iron features, immitagable to all the rest of mankind, they see only benignity and love, is but a spectrum of the very priest himself, projected upon the surrounding darkness.

In "The Beast in the Jungle" John Marcher, like Hollingsworth, is obsessed in constructing his intellectualized design around *one aspect* of existence: the crouching beast which will spring at him in the future. Because he is so driven by his extreme rationalism, he can only live in a shallow, destructive manner. The end of the *nouvelle* captures the tension of head and heart.

Believing that his design (of distinction) has not been worth the effort, Marcher returns to May's grave and notes the passion of another mourner. "Marcher knew him at once for one of the deeply stricken—a perception as sharp that nothing else in the picture comparatively lived." This epiphany reveals "with a pang" to him that he has neither suffered nor lived: "He has seen *outside* of his life." He had believed in false forms which neglect the ravages within. And like Isabel Archer's "visitation," the illumination compels John Marcher to rebel against his mechanized way of life; he has to *do something*. Unlike Isabel, however, he must be content with the embrace of death: he must fling himself on the tomb. He cannot begin a *vita nuova*—that is the problem. "The Beast had lurked indeed, and the Beast, at its hour, had sprung." We can say, in conclusion, that his over-intellectualized design, built on the premise that the Beast was a thing to be awaited, had neglected the sudden spring of Life. Life and death are consequently merged at May's tomb.

Our seven writers draw upon their complex, dual heritage. It is not my task here to explore their sources. Have they used "The Beast in the Jungle" or *Moby Dick* or *Huckleberry Finn*? Have they been influenced by the Talmudic exchanges or Yiddish proverbs? Such questions, although useful, may get in the way of the real "moment": our writers assume that every Jew (and American) must confront the tension between head and heart before he can find himself and God. They believe that over-intellectualization is "sinful"; it is responsible for exile, unholy family life, and "bad times."

Although Karl Shapiro deals with the tension between intellect and feeling in many of his poems and essays, I want here to look closely at one long poem, "Adam and Eve." [12]

The first section, entitled "The Sickness of Adam," begins with Adam's turning toward the East: he praises the "nature of things." Why does he? What compels his adoration? Is it instinct or reason? Shapiro makes it clear that Adam is moved *instinctively*. But once our "primitive" father learns every path, once he finds himself lost in habit, he cannot be instinctive. His intellect gets in the way. "Thinking became a garden of its own." This garden is fertile and dangerous: although it has new things—words, beasts of the imagination—it inhibits his fresh responses. He is slightly morose. He even contemplates departure. Because Adam is torn by terrifying self-division, he is, in a sense, dead. He "falls down with labor." It is now that God approaches in the cool of the day; He will invigorate him by creating Eve.

In the second section, "The Recognition of Eve," we see the woman who has just been born. She stares at the new world and turns toward Adam. When their eyes meet, their feelings assert themselves. Words are unimportant; only the senses matter: "she raised her hand / And touched his wound where it was fading now, / For he must feel the place to understand." Of course, Adam thinks about Eve's strangeness, but his thoughts disappear while he watches her gestures. And in the third section, "The Kiss," their happiness results from openness to feeling, to passion. They dance—Adam was in the beginning, a "temple dancer." But in their dance, they are dimly conscious of the "Tree of Guilt," some *thing* rustling overhead. And after their fourth caress, they hide.

Section four, "The Tree of Guilt," tells us about inhibition. Instead of listening to the oracle of Love—to the "Tree of Life"—Eve hurries to that other Tree—of Guilt. She learns somehow that Love is evil. Is Shapiro saying that this is true? Or is he saying that rationalism is evil? Eve seems to be guilt-ridden because she limits her instinctive gestures: mystery is abandoned; Love is torn by thought. The serpent is the deity of rationalism, using it to confuse Eve. Consequently in the next section, "The Confession," she informs her husband that *they* are the garden; her knowledge distorts the situation, affirming *and* denying the worth of feeling. She thinks too much; she manipulates him. Lies—intentional or unintentional—dominate their first climax.

Section six, "Shame," repeats the preceding tensions. The shadow of fear—gained by false knowledge—destroys Love. Adam and Eve see "the covering that reveals," the mask of truth. *They become animals, not because they lack understanding, but because they possess unnatural, non-instinctive reasons.* And their "Exile"—the title of the last section—is from each other and Paradise. They are in the "present world"—separated from their own instincts; they survive as divided creatures.

The tension between head and heart is Shapiro's chief concern now. It enters his literary criticism. In an essay entitled "What is Not Poetry?" (reprinted in *In Defense of Ignorance*) he writes, "The rational person is least able to understand poetry. Or rather, it is his understanding of it that prevents him from seeing it as anything but a series of words in meters, with various rhetorical devices and 'levels' of meaning." (Surely the "knowledge" of Adam and Eve prevents them from seeing Love.) Elsewhere in the essay he condemns the intellectual "forcing of one's way toward reality." Modern Poetry is mechanistic, highly rational, and dangerous. In a related essay entitled "Farmer and Poet" (in *Poetry*, XCVIII, 170–85) Shapiro juxtaposes two "types"—Adam and Eve *before* and *after* the Tree of Guilt?—"To the living biologic man, whether poet or farmer, life does not require a meaning. Life is its own meaning. It has no other goal other than its own functioning. To the mechanical man life is a series of laws and compulsions, fiats and decalogues." Although we may question his somewhat simple typology, we cannot fail to admire Shapiro's courageous rebellion against the dehumanization of man.[13]

Heinz Politzer has written that Delmore Schwartz' "creative atmosphere is the light of consciousness, which he flashes upon the obscure reality of his memories." [14] Consciousness often conflicts with feeling; this clash is evident in *Genesis*.

The opening lines express the conflict: Hershey Green is almost thoughtless, free of mental "anguish." But his "conscious mind snaps up!" Consciousness turns away and comes back; it is obsessive, disturbing, and "necessary." He cannot do without it, although he would like to rest in peace. Neither can he wholly enjoy his feelings; they nourish his consciousness. Hershey is grasped by tension; he cannot sleep; he is trapped. Now "voices" call out to him. "Hallucination leads you by the hand." They are here to "test" him and, if possible, to give him the strength to heal his divided being. The long conversation that follows is a debate between intellect and feeling.

Hershey tells his life-story, going back to his Euro-

pean ancestors. He "remembers" the lives of his grand-
parents (reliving them). He sees motives, necessities,
and desires. He tries to "understand" the relative
strengths of conciousness and conscience, intellect
and feeling. The voices aren't helpful: at times they
respond to his narration by stressing the primacy of
intellect; then they contradict themselves (and one
another). Thus one says, "I only meant that knowledge was a joy / A painful joy perhaps, and yet what
else." But another says (after Hershey reaches his own
childhood), "The ego as the ego makes the world /
Glass! glass infinitely divisible: / The ego sees itself in
every place / Reflected as if Nature were Versailles' /
Reflexive halls and walls!—"Intellect is joyful and
obsessive. And feeling? Can it remain free of contami-
nation? Can it respond innocently? Again we find
contradictions. Hershey as child instinctively flees
from the anti-semitic janitor, but he immediately
wants to know what "Jew" means; he *needs abstractions*. When he later hears Mrs. Rinehart, his
mother's Gentile neighbor, rage against him, the scene
is so shocking that it can never leave him. Feelings
remain undefined—as vague guilt—but once they are
defined, they become even more burdensome.

Pain results from the debate between Hershey and
the voices (who are, after all, *his* conflicting desires
and thoughts). He learns that "Man's Nature is this
being-in-the-world, / this in-ness is the warmest thing
in Life." In-ness is always split.

Although Schwartz has recently abandoned this
kind of introspection—he does not, for example, write
such a poem as "The Heavy Bear Who Goes With
Me Now" or such a novelette as "The World is a
Wedding"—he still deals with "head and heart."
"Successful Love" is a good example of his new fiction.
Susan Calhoun is a complete innocent—imagine her

conversing with Hershey Green! Her feelings dominate her; they make her respond "freshly": Daddy is
the "darlingest dear"; Mummy is "really keen." She
doesn't want to resemble her father because as she tells
us, "if you thought too much about things, you never
had any fun." We would expect Schwartz to be spiteful towards Susan (and her culture), but he makes us
see that Daddy, Roger Calhoun, is ill-equipped to
handle his daughter's romance. His "knowledge" exiles him from the modern world: "how much farther
in the brave new world of 1950 would he go before
getting to the sanctuary and ancient castle of his own
home?"

The title refers to the sex-manual read by Susan
(and then by her father). She really believes, without
thinking, that there are easy roads to any kind of
success, and when her fiancé goes into the Army, she
simply exchanges him for another. She is not lost; she
thrives with clichés. When Roger Calhoun reads the
manual, he notes this line. "Although it is not ordi-
narily thought of as such, the mind is the first of the
erogenous zones." He laughs. But he gradually realizes
that he has always separated intellect from feeling,
demanding "perfect" knowledge in himself and others. The sentence haunts him; in its ridiculous way it
emphasizes unity: people *do* respond instinctively—
these responses are probably as valid as any other,
especially in this crazy, new world. "It might be true
that most human beings are much simpler than one
commonly supposes them to be; one is oneself far
simpler than one often supposes. But it was also true
that the simple were extremely complicated. He felt
entirely lost in the terror and jungle of innocence."

Schwartz is thus proclaiming the good fortune of
innocence. But we wonder whether Susan's "fabulous" lack of consciousness is really so wonderful. We

side with Hershey Green and his painful consciousness.

Isaac Rosenfeld was constantly tortured.

> To acknowledge one's instinctual life, to educate the
> feelings, to be thoroughly onto oneself, to struggle
> against the pettiness and defensiveness and prevar-
> ications of the ego for the larger claims and possi-
> bilities of existence, to understand the enormity of
> the modern world's encroachments upon the natural
> and individual life and oppose them by the force of
> one's desires and intelligence and hope—so [he]
> continued to live and write.[15]

Let us look first at his fiction. In a parable published
in *Partisan Review* (June, 1948), he describes a government clerk who, seeking advancement, decides to
make a good impression. He shaves, in preparation for
an interview with his superior, but he cannot simply
shave his cheek. He *reasons* that he should *really*
shave; he shaves his entire body—until he is too late
for the interview. Then he cuts his throat. What does
this strange parable—worthy of Kafka himself—
mean? Rosenfeld tells us. Not only does he give us one
meaning, but many different ones. Like his clerk, he
can't stop rationalizing: consciousness plagues him.
And as he proceeds, he realizes this similarity, using
the parable (and its explanation) to question the
relative merits of learning and instinct, head and
heart. "Isn't there a point where our subtlety becomes
too fine for itself, and what we write consciously, by
calculation, becomes all the greater an unconscious
act? I wrote this parable with its moral neither before
me nor behind me; I wrote it understanding and not
understanding what it means." The line between understanding and non-understanding fascinates him—
afraid of intellectualization and drawn to it, he cap-

tures this tension by quoting Pascal. "To make light of philosophy is to be a true philosopher."

The parable illuminates the more "familiar" stories. Consider "The Hand that Fed Me." Joseph Feigenbaum, as we have seen, is so "conscious" that he finds unnecessary meaning in a trivial event, making it much bigger than it should be. There is profound irony when he writes to Ellen, "Trivialites are the things women rush into, feeling they're important." Doesn't *he* do this? Yet at the same time Feigenbaum admires feeling, instinct, and spontaneity: the way Ellen looks when she holds a pencil; his immediate love for her: "Love pre-exists in the heart." Perhaps the clearest statement of these tensions is made in the last letter when he writes that some men rise "out of their own lives": "Their only secret is a tremendous willingness—they do not struggle with themselves!"

Of course, we could also discuss Bernard in these terms—doesn't he struggle with himself by *planning* to be free?—but perhaps an even better example of Rosenfeld's polarization is in "The Colony," an early, prize-winning novelette (*Partisan Review*, Winter, 1945.) Satya, the leader of the rebels delivers a speech; while he stares at his many followers, he thinks, "Yet, knowing their misery, their humiliation, recognizing signs of disease, malnourishment and deformity, knowing also the ignorance of the people, he felt himself withdrawn, *observing where he should have been moved to participation through sympathy*" [my italics]. He contrasts himself to Bapu, the former leader, who "never suffered the complexities of a divided nature." And the government responds to Satya's speech by putting him in prison—his cell symbolizes not only the totalitarian state but his own nature. He is trapped by his thoughts which compel him to analyze his feelings, corrupting these very feelings. Satya tries to soothe his troubled spirit: he "visualizes" saintliness; he longs for unity. His diary entries—how often Rosenfeld uses these!—express his problems. "Polarity, the whole of life. Woe to them who live fully." "Victory is not only over enemy. Is over ourselves!" Does Satya resolve his polarities? At one point he thinks, "the whole person, with all his imperfections and the whole ideal life, with all its austerities—the two were in harmony, even though one hand did not know what the other was doing." But at the end of the story Satya finally achieves "saintliness," watching his fellow prisoners beat him. "His pain and pity [are] identical." He is no longer divided because "now suffering alone constituted his hold in life."

Theodore Solotaroff tells us that Rosenfeld's "appeal as a critic, comes in good part from the ability— rare in modern criticism—to make one *care*." [16] He makes us care because he challenges our divided natures; he refers constantly to head and heart, condemning those writers who disregard this inevitable (for him) duality. Thus Nancy Hale's "sensibility is formal"; it lacks passion. Her fiction serves as an example of the well-made story which he tells us, in another essay, ignores the "structure of character"— the "obsession of the personal." Philosophical Naturalism is the "failure of verve"—it dismisses yearning as "an illegitimate form of inference." Rosenfeld, of course, admires Kafka: "with Kafka it is the function of sensibility to provide precisely the perception of generality." The intellect and the heart are united (as they are divided) in his work. Kafka is not another Charles Williams who deals intellectually with Christianity but never makes his readers experience it. Rosenfeld desires Incarnation—*thought made flesh*.

Leslie Fiedler also deals with the tension between

head and heart. His heroes are usually conscious designers who neglect their feelings. They are as obsessive as Shenandoah Fish or Joseph Feigenbaum.

When Milton, the narrator of "Pull Down Vanity!" arrives at the summer institute to teach creative
writing, he invents a new self. It pleases him to mystify
the others who cannot believe that he has seven
children! But the danger of such self-creation is that it
arises from innocence—Milton has succumbed to conscious planning to the point where it is all he possesses.
Thus he is obsessive. (Obsession is the dark side of
innocence.) He is challenged and destroyed by reality.
Judith, the wife of a graduate student, falls for him—
or, rather, for his intellectualized, compulsive design.
She forces him to react emotionally—to love her or
not. But Milton is afraid—such freshness is no longer
part of him. He can only continue to obey his other
self. He refuses to love Judith—she is, after all, a
Gentile! Jew and Gentile—and other abstractions—
save his innocence. The irony is that he cannot *believe*
in them; they are used only to cover himself a bit
more.

"Nude Croquet" is often dismissed as a "shocking"
story—*Esquire* did publish it!—but it is more than
that. It presents a group of people, who, like the
"creative" Milton, have divorced intellect from feeling. Each believes in some design (but not whole-
heartedly) which protects him. Such innocent belief
substitutes unreality for reality. Howard "snarls ritu-
ally" in the first line of the story and this ritualistic
snarl introduces us to the other perverse, *conscious*
rituals adopted by his aging friends. All snarl at reality;
all are "masked with iron filigree"—like the house in
which they meet. Gradually these innocents lose their
rigidity. Their consciousness blurs; their destructive
patterns disintegrate. Molly, the young wife, decides

to startle the old "gang" by undressing. Nudity, for her, is purity of being—an antidote to over-intel-lectualization. The others agree to her idea of nude croquet, although Marvin says, "It would be more to the point to put on steel masks and lead drawers, to hide in all decency a nakedness we can no longer pretend is exciting or beautiful." What Molly doesn't realize is that pure feeling—or spontaneity—is as irritating and dangerous as pure intellect. The two must exist dialectically; when separated, each corrupts the soul. The story ends dramatically: Marvin, the spokes-man for unity (opposing "romantic nudity"), dies of a heart attack; Molly sees his body and knows "for the first time what it meant to be really nude."

"The Dancing of Reb Hershl with the Withered Hand" is set in a small Jewish community. One day a dead Gentile child is found; the citizens expect a pogrom and they hide "the five men in whom was vested the wisdom of the Community." Thus we are led to expect "the sayings of the fathers." These five men are bookish. Reb Nahum, for example, dislikes Moishe, their vulgar driver: "An irreverent idiot." They are proud of their learning, often quoting from the Talmud. They do not expect miracles to happen to them.

Moishe, however, disturbs the rabbis' smart discus-sions. Who is he? Is he simply an idiot driver or— Elijah? The meeting of the driver and the wise men turns on the duality I have been tracing. Moishe teaches them that the "end of reason is to know the limits of reason, all right reasoning must close in on itself, making a circle which is Zero or God!" Reason is useless: the causes of the death of the Gentile child (and of the destruction of the Egyptians in the past) cannot be known. Only revelation captures truth. Miracles occur to affirm the uselessness of mere learning. After the Gentile child is resurrected, after the five men hear Elijah, after the signs have been given—the wise men realize the utter mystery of existence. When Reb Hershl dances holding aloft his withered hand (the work of the driver), he touches the center of all meaning. "But whether that meaning was joy or sorrow, knowledge or bafflement, or some strange marriage of them all, it would have been difficult to say."

In *Love and Death in the American Novel* Fiedler suggests that our literature is Gothic because it deals with the Faustian archetype (in all of its manifestations). Faust is obsessively involved with knowledge; he sells his soul—his capacity for feelings?—to the Devil. He becomes a monster.

> It is because they come to terms so frankly with the Faustian implications of their own enterprise that writers like Melville and Hawthorne (later Twain and Faulkner, too) are able to create Faustian characters, satisfy the dimly perceived need of many Americans to have their national existence projected in terms of a compact with the Devil. In Hawthorne, the scientist and the social reformer; in Melville, the ruthless exploiter of nature and the magnetic leader of men; in Twain, the refugee from culture, the young man who goes West; in Faulkner, the self-made man fighting for status and security—in each, some standard and respected American type is identified with the black magician who bartered away his soul.

Faustian aspiration, for Fiedler, replaces the "passionate encounter of man and woman in our books" (to quote Benjamin DeMott).[17] Underneath American affirmations lies an "incapacity to envisage the wholeness of a human being in any fashion not crippling either to physicality on the one hand or to intelligence on the other."[18] Of course, Fiedler does slant the issue—"innocently" using his intelligence—but it is characteristic of him to do this: he is haunted by the mystery of knowledge. Does knowledge lie in the head or the heart (or both)? He never does answer this question, but by showing us the danger of "bifurcation," of obsessive masquerade, he points the way.

Saul Bellow is also troubled by the compulsive design which neglects sympathy and joy. His fiction deals with the "madness" of over-intellectualization.

We find it in *The Victim*. Allbee treats Asa as an *object of play*: he knows about his wife's trip, his departure from work earlier in the day. He believes that *Asa as Jew is evil; he is to blame for everything wrong in the world*. To fight chaos he accepts this paranoid view; it enhances his self-image, giving him "secret" knowledge. Of course, Bellow does not give us a black and white picture. Asa is equally prepared to consider the other man as evil—an evil *Gentile*. He regards Allbee's constant play as "some freakish, insane process." It's the only way he can keep himself intact—at all powerful. The two designers battle each other.

Schlossberg is one of the few sane people in New York. Unlike the others—Allbee, Asa, Rudiger—he understands that ideal constructions, cruel abstractionism, narcissistic values rob men of their humanity.

Schlossberg begins his discussion by remarking that a certain actress is not human—merely "lame." She does not show in her face "fear, hate, a hard heart, cruelness, fascination." She is mechanical—so much so that "she is not a woman." Her actions parallel the mad actions of the main characters. Then Schlossberg generalizes. "Everything comes in packages. If it's in a package, you can bring the devil in the house." Humanity itself has become a commodity, something wrapped up, not allowed to flourish. Madness takes away our potentialities. There is brutal irony: Asa and Allbee are "less than human" because they have tried—especially Allbee—to be "more than human," to be godlike in their ideal constructions. Schlossberg returns to his opening remarks. "Good acting is what is exactly human."

The Adventures of Augie March also presents madness. On the very first page we see that Grandma Lausch governs Augie, Simon, Georgie, and Mama, informing them that they must act craftily at the Charities office. Although Grandma proclaims that she is merely helping them—"You see how it is—do I have to say more? There's no man in the house and children to bring up"—she is taking away their ability to choose, their risk-filled humanity. Miraculously Augie remains "larky and boisterous." But he finds other "mad crusaders." Anna Coblin says, "I'll treat you like my own boy . . . my own Howard." "Love" again comes into focus, but Anna's love regards Augie as an abstraction—a substitute-son. After all, anyone would do. Einhorn, like the two mothers, adopts Augie: he had a "teaching turn similar to Grandma Lausch's, both believing they could show what could be done with the world, where it gave or resisted, where you could be confident." Later Mrs. Renling too has a "mission," seeing that "there was something adoptional" about Augie—she offers him new clothing.

Bellow takes a new view of madness. He looks at it with humor. Here are two related examples. Einhorn decides that he will teach Augie about women; he takes him to a cat-house. The humor arises from the fact that crippled Einhorn has to be *carried* by Augie; teacher and student, "designer" and "thing," play reverse roles. Bellow implies by this upside-down view that "strong" lovers are slaves of compulsive, over-intellectualized narcissism.

Mrs. Renling is an "eternal" builder. The juxtaposition of her silliness and Roman greatness—of two different designs—makes Augie laugh. Mrs. Renling is not so "paranoid" as Allbee, but her madness reflects the madness of the entire system.

It is surprising that most critics mention Augie's joyous lack of commitments, without underlining the tension he has between remaining free and building ideal constructions, between his head and heart. Robert Gorham Davis discusses his "involvement and detachment" but neglects the foster-home dream—an *involvement* of self.[19] Robert Penn Warren explains that Augie is the "man with no commitments." [20] This kind of remark is "easy," robbing Bellow of irony. Not only does he present the ideal academy—he shows us that Augie is "obsessively" aware of freedom. This "faithfulness to his image of himself as free"—to quote Chester Eisinger—becomes ideal, abstract, and compulsive.[21] When Augie talks at great length about freedom, he reminds us of Isabel Archer—who proclaims her independence but marries Gilbert Osmond. But Bellow somehow seems less detached than James. He favors Augie's ideal, without completely noting its inadequacies. Surely there is truth in Bergler's remarks about the novel: Bellow does avoid explaining the reason for obsessive involvement with no commitments.[22] Augie remains a curious, shadowy figure who runs away from himself and us.

There is madness in *Seize the Day*. Dr. Tamkin maintains that he *knows* how to beat the system—his investment scheme (which he compels Tommy to join) is based on the fact that he has more sense than other investors. He is, in other words, a complete narcissist, who regards poor Tommy as a kind of sport. Again Bellow is ironic. This mad crusader is "calm and rational," but he loses this rationality because he constantly thinks of it—it becomes something over which he has no control. His first words to Tommy are, "You have a very obsessional look on your face." His statement is true—at least *we* know it applies to almost all of Bellow's characters—but it is true *only* because Tamkin always sees "obsessional looks"— except on *his* face. He thinks, "every public figure had a character-neurosis. Maddest of all were the businessmen, the heartless, flaunting, boisterous business class who ruled this country with their hard manners and their bold lies and their absurd words that nobody could believe." The doctor regards the world as a patient, projecting his own illness. His designs, theories, and games help to make Tamkin important. At the same time they take away his power and feelings. When he speaks about the world, we should listen carefully. Regard this statement: "all suicide is murder, and all murder is suicide." Most critics have discussed his murder of Tommy, but they have not seen his suicidal constructions.

There is some truth in Tamkin's remarks. Dr. Adler, Tommy's father, is also imprisoned in his own designs. He believes that money or "style" means more than love. Because his son is a failure, he cannot accept him—in fact, he rejects him at every turn. This is done to assert correctness, knowledge, and power. But Dr. Adler praises his children to outsiders—after all, *they* don't know his true feelings. He says, consequently, that his daughter, now married, once had an "important position in Mount Sinai." Tommy becomes a success. Underneath his smile, Dr. Adler has lost the "family sense."

Caught between two designers, Tommy wants to

shape some ideal construction. Because he has never known one, he views his limitations as all-important. He is in love with failure. It is wonderfully ironic that Tommy courts successive losses—in marriage, in his occupation, in his family—in the midst of other crusaders for success. His construction objectifies the actions of Dr. Tamkin and Dr. Adler; his masochism reflects their sadism. But he learns that failure is not the only ideal. He gains self-knowledge by learning about his own heart. He cries.

Bernard Malamud affirms the polarities of head and heart. In "The Last Mohican" Fidelman, the "self-confessed failure as a painter," comes to Rome with his "new pigskin leather brief case." He wishes only to capture historical truth. But his "learning"—his rigid personality—has never been tested. When he meets Susskind, the deceptive beggar, he does not know what to do with him. This stranger upsets his obsessive, "careful" designs, forcing him to admit the chaos of life and the necessity of compassion. Their first conversation turns on the question of fulfilment.

> Susskind glanced down at his shabby, baggy knickers. "I haven't had a suit for years. The one I was wearing when I ran away from Germany, fell apart. One day I was walking around naked."
>
> "Isn't there a welfare organization that could help you out—some group in the Jewish community, interested in refugees?"
>
> "The only thing they offer me is a ticket back to Israel."
>
> "Why don't you take it?"
>
> "I told you already, here I feel free."
>
> "Freedom is a relative term."
>
> "Don't tell me about freedom."

Fidelman believes in institutions, absolutes, and convenient categories—"tightly organized" life. Susskind sees through such belief, claiming that life is more than easy thought.

The story continues this dialectic. Although Fidelman gets himself quickly organized—he arranges a "schedule"—he does not seem to "live." He fears history, Rome, his own feelings. Susskind becomes his troublesome "angel": he is out for his own well-being—stealing, gossiping, and malingering—but his angelic power lies in his ability to make Fidelman less automatic—more human. He makes him assume responsibility for all exiles (including himself). After a while Fidelman's pattern is fragmented: he can't sleep; he can't constrict his feelings. He searches for Susskind, consciously hoping to get back his stolen brief case, but secretly longing for new "knowledge." He gains this new knowledge in the Jewish cemetery which, unlike the picturesque churches, is close to his ambivalent being. Here he recognizes the horrible crimes caused by automation of personality. He eventually locates Susskind, who tells him that he has burned his manuscript, asserting that this outrage is really a "favor." And so it is. It compels Fidelman to see his own limitations and to cry wisely.

"The Mourners" deals in a less sophisticated way with the same dialectical pattern. Kessler lives alone (another ghetto!); he has adopted an obsessive style which corrupts his total response to life. But even this "monster" is human; he demands some sympathy. Although we side with Gruber, the landlord, who is reasonably irritated by Kessler's spiteful actions, we learn that *he* is also inflexible—he refuses to accept his tenant's humanity. When Gruber sees Kessler mourning—for him!—he almost has a stroke. Then he grabs Kessler's sheet, drapes his head with it, and becomes another "mourner." Mourning challenges rigidity. Does it win?

In the recent collection of stories, *Idiots First*, we again encounter Arthur Fidelman. No longer is he the conscious designer; he is slowly adjusting to his greater humanity. He is more playful—another Susskind?— he takes more chances. "Still Life" gives us this Fidelman. When he meets Annamaria Oliovino, the pittrice, he cannot contain his feelings: "it can't be, he thought in desperation, but it could." Although he labors to "extricate his fate from hers, he [is] already a plucked bird, greased, and ready for frying." But he still tries to do his work. (It is interesting that he is a painter here, rather than an art critic. Are critics less flexible?) He is almost too sympathetic to survive: his feelings—about Annamaria, about life in general— dominate him.

"The Evil Eye" which is at the heart of the story creates "still life." The pittrice has accepted a superstitious pattern; it makes her act less freely than her feelings demand. It swings her from fear to anger. Annamaria and Fidelman are, in a sense, "Evil Eyes," obliquely gazing at the world. But they do *see clearly* at the end. Their insight comes when they let themselves go. Their bodies are reborn—still life is abandoned—as Fidelman, wearing the priest's vestments, embraces Annamaria, nailing "her to the cross." This inverted ritual is deliberately shocking. Malamud suggests that only a spiritual explosion can shatter institutionalized, rigid habit—new life is gained through risky, joyous "pumping."

Philip Roth deals less successfully with head and heart. He opposes abstract learning, but he is too "clever" to embrace spontaneity. Perhaps he is not really unusual in this respect: Schwartz is, after all, less "artificial" in *Genesis* than in "Successful Love"; the joy in *The Adventures of Augie March* is abstract; the old Fidelman is more interesting than his new self.

"Defender of the Faith" demonstrates Roth's dilemma. It deals with mercy and justice, feeling and intellectualization. The narrator, Sergeant Marx, tells us that he "had been fortunate enough to develop an infantryman's heart which like his feet, at first aches and swells, but finally grows horny enough for him to travel the weirdest paths without feeling a thing." Such containment enabled him to survive the war; can it help him live in peace? If Marx is very abstract, his double, Grossbart, is full of feeling. Both are still born—to use Malamud's metaphor: Marx must dominate life through conscious planning; Grossbart must assert himself through self-pity. The two men clash. Marx realizes that Grossbart plays with his Jewish Feeling, but he will not let himself change. He sways slightly, allowing the private (and his two buddies) to take advantage of him. "Out of the many recollections that had tumbled over me these past few days, I heard from some childhood moment my grandmother's voice: 'What are you making a tsimas?' " But at the end, he makes a *tsimas*—to protect his inflexible design. When he punishes Grossbart, he calls it justice triumphing over mercy. But we wonder: Is Grossbart merely his scapegoat? Perhaps Marx punishes him because he cannot acknowledge his own "grossness," his own humanity.

The epigraph to *Goodbye, Columbus* is a Yiddish proverb. "The heart is half a prophet." Roth uses it to suggest that feeling is so uncontrollable that it can prevent complete understanding: pity becomes self-pity; pure emotion becomes sentimentality. The line between healthy and sick feeling is very thin; we need courage and reason to walk it. Eli and Ozzie, the "mad crusaders," find wisdom in "letting go"; Sergeant Marx, Neil Klugman, and Gabe Wallach, on the other hand, condemn such surrender to feeling. Roth has not yet decided where he stands. Because he is so *conscious* of the "dialectical" line, he walks very carefully at times.

"The heart is half a prophet"; "What are you making a *tsimas*"; "But if you chose to be crazy, then you weren't crazy!"; "The heart is law!"—these lines (from Roth's stories) represent the urgent needs of head and heart in Jewish-American literature. They are not answers; they are only dialectical possibilities.

HESCHEL TELLS US that the "craving for God has never subsided in the Jewish soul." [1] Perhaps Psalm 42 expresses it most poetically.

> *As a hart yearns for the streams of water,*
> *So does my soul yearn for Thee, O God.*
> *My soul thirsts for God, the living God,*
> *When shall I come and see the face of the Lord.*

But how does the Jew find Him? Heschel suggests three traditional ways: worship, learning, and action. [2] "The three are one, and we must go all three ways to reach the one destination. For this is what Israel discovered: the God of nature is the God of history, and the way to know Him is to do His will." [3]

Our seven writers crave God, but they do not seek Him through orthodox worship, learning, and action. They are more "solitary": because they are torn by dualities—exile and Land, head and heart, past and present—they believe that God is the Transcendence of such dualities. In trying to identify this Transcendence, they point everywhere—at sex, nature, joy—and although they do not eventually accept the Jewish God, they do give us a "legacy of wonder" and "mystery." [4]

Heschel maintains that "among the many things

that religious tradition holds in store for us is *a legacy of wonder*. The surest way to suppress our ability to understand the meaning of God and the importance of worship is *to take things for granted*." [5] Surely our writers are not indifferent; the fact that they suffer dualities signifies their lack of indifference. *They do wonder.* Occasionally their wonder is negative: How can life be so absurd? But from this position they move dialectically to Positive Wonder (which rises above absurd questioning). And they sense mystery, affirming, like Ecclesiastes, "That which *is, is far off and deep, exceedingly deep*." Being is mysterious for them.

In his introduction to *Poems of a Jew* Karl Shapiro writes, "Judaism is the minimum religion . . . . The unbelievable survival of the Jews must be seen against a background of Nothing, a people outside art or literature, a people in dread of the graven image, a people outside a Heaven and Hell, whose very sanctum sanctorum is an empty chamber." Because Judaism is so "minimum" (for him), it points to the "very center of the divine manifestation— man." He seems to relate the Jew to humanism. But when we look at some of the poems, we see that they express deep longing for Transcendence.

"The Tingling Back," for example, deals with momentary sensations of God. It begins with the narrator "deeply immured" in his literary work, alone with his "own smoke," not conscious of his body. "Swiftly" he feels an "angry shower" of arrows upon his back; these arrows are like electric needles "run amok / between . . . flesh and shirt." What is this electricity? Is it simply, as the narrator believes, the "pain" of something he said or did the other day? No. It is the pain of separation from God. In the last lines he seems to change his ground—the "tingling back" moves him from self-scrutiny—studying his "sincerity like a crime . . ."—to scrutiny of God. He affirms unconsciously that his actions can be valid in relation to some Higher Being. Of course, the narrator remains worldy, but his tingling (or rather his *awareness* of this tingling) is perhaps a hint of divinity asserting itself.

Shapiro finds Transcendence in sex. "The Confirmation" counterpoises masturbation to divinity. While parents worship their God, the boy worships his own body. His masturbation ritualistically affirms some life force which is as "spiritual" as an "otherworldly" figure. His "perfect consciousness of joy" is, in effect, Transcendent. But is this equation wise? Shapiro apparently believes that the boy (humanity?) can only find divinity in himself; such tingling is all there is. The problem is that "perfect consciousness of joy" is usually mixed with—and destroyed by—guilt. Adam and Eve in the long poem I have already mentioned lose paradise—which is within their bodies—because they submit to thinking—to habit. They are, in effect, less divine than the boy. Shapiro is thus torn by the duality of guilt and joy in sex. In some unconscious way he associates sex with divinity, but he is uneasy with this association as in "The First Time," a poem in which the prostitue asks the unsure, virginal boy, "*Are you a Jew?*" Thus Shapiro must "overcompensate," picturing sex in the most exaggerated way until it becomes as unreal (or non-human) as orthodox religion—according to him. Perhaps we can put his problem in this way. He is so troubled by dualistic thinking that he cannot fully embrace Transcendence. Sex, he knows, is often painful *and* joyous; so is the "tingling back." But he cannot consciously accept this ambivalence because it harms his scheme. Shapiro fools himself into believing that Sex is One.

Does he believe in God? Yes. His God is described

as "Cosmic Consciousness": "By cosmic consciousness is meant the capacity of the individual consciousness to experience a sense of total unity with all
Nature, or the universe, or some degree of that experience." ("Science-mysticism" is another term he uses
in *In Defense of Ignorance*.) Shapiro is illogical here.
How can the *conscious* individual who is troubled by
polarities rise above them; how can he *sense* total
unity? Simply by not thinking? But how does he do
that? By responding to his body-feelings? Shapiro
moves in circles. Of course, he would suggest that such
circular movement is necessary; he would quote from
Zen, Wilhelm Reich, Henry Miller, and Jung.
It is ironic that he has finally substituted a "low"
religion for Judaism. His God is "Cosmic Consciousness" (usually through sex or real poetry); his Bible is
the authors mentioned above, his tradition is his own
life-style. But this new religion is phony because it is
built on individual consciousness which finds it difficult (as he has shown in his own strife-torn poetry) to
heal self-division—an inevitable fact of humanity.
There *is* a line between fathers and sons, past and
present, whether Shapiro likes to think of it or not.

Delmore Schwartz has also moved toward Transcendence of polarities. His recent collection, *Summer Knowledge: New and Selected Poems 1938–
1958*, contains such sections as "Morning Bells,"
"The Phoenix Choir," and "The Fulfillment"; in
these he emphasizes natural growth, rebirth, newness,
and unity—what Shapiro would call "cosmic consciousness."

"Summer Knowledge" contains the most complete
statement of Schwartz' Transcendence. It opens with
these lines. "Summer knowledge is not the winter's
truth, the truth of fall, / the autumn's fruition, vision,
and recognition." Already we see the transformation:

the characteristic narrator has been replaced by a prophet who speaks musically. Although he describes contraries—summer knowledge as opposed to "winter's truth" and "autumn's fruition"—he is not unbalanced by them; he sees them as part of a neverending, disciplined cycle. Even black torment and the first knowledge of pain *belong* to Nature. But they are not as profound as "summer knowledge" which is the "supple recognition of the fullness and the fatness and the roundness of ripeness." The prophet sees the ripeness of things; his vision is not momentary (as it perhaps would be in an early poem by Schwartz)—it dominates the rest of the poem. What is the ripeness? Where does it come from? Such questions may trouble us (as they do with Shapiro's Transcendence), but they don't prevent the prophet from repeating, not logically clarifying, his ecstatic statements. He tells us that summer knowledge is not "the knowledge of love and learning." It is, on the contrary, "cat knowledge, deer knowledge." Humanity, nature, death, and birth—all "dance" together in the "knowledge before and after knowledge." Schwartz thus reaches the position in one Zen poem quoted by Shapiro. "No thought, no reflection, no analysis, / No cultivation, no intention; / Let it settle itself."

The very form of "Summer Knowledge" is Transcendent. In contrast to his earlier syllogistic poems, this one doesn't follow "strictness." Its center is "Summer Knowledge"; around this phrase are mystical lights—"flowering, rebirth," "Death"—and present participles which suggest *fulfilling* cycles. Repetitions abound. The poem is as circular and "natural" as an apple. But the one defect which Schwartz cannot avoid is also apparent: "Summer Knowledge" is a bit dull, once we ask for meaning in (or behind) the music. After we stop responding to the cosmic dance, we realize that there is something make-believe about it. *We have been seduced into not thinking.* Schwartz would probably claim that this is his very intention: he wants, like some Higher Being, to lift us out of our "meddling intellect"—the Wordsworthian phrase. We stand again close to the heart of the matter: Is such Transcendence real or artificial?

In his recent stories Schwartz is not interested in motivation, strictness of plot, or credibility. Only co-incidence, miracle, and extra-logical motivations fascinate him. The change has bothered several critics (who have not noted its relation to "Summer Knowledge"). Robert W. Flint complains that Schwartz has "turned to writing the sort of fable that has become increasingly popular," one which does not give us life itself.[6] Irving Howe believes that the recent stories are "not quite so good as his earlier work," although he thinks they are still "the work of an important and gifted writer, whose voice is uniquely his own."[7]

"The Gift" is perhaps the best of these stories. It deals with young Toby's visit to Brooklyn for Martha's birthday—to the "borough where he was born so long ago he could not remember." He does not have a gift; his parents decided only this morning to let him travel alone. But in the childhood world—childhood, not adolescence, is summer knowledge—wonderful coincidences happen. After Toby prays to God, he gets into a cab which hits another one. He cries. The policeman arrives, gives him the gift he had wanted to give his own daughter, and makes him calm once more. Isn't this good fortune? Isn't this fabulous? Isn't this gift a sign of God? Toby thinks, "It might be dangerous to pray for presents but anyway he was sure now that there was a God."

"An American Fairy Tale" opens with these lines. "This is a fairy tale. And it is a success story. It is a story which is not only full of goodness and beauty, but it is also a true story. It is full of purity, innocence, and happiness." Purity, innocence, happiness, success—Schwartz gives us in this story and the others heroes who are "down and out" at the beginning and miraculously successful at the end. They find "colossal fortune" in the invisible unity of events. They are graced with summer knowledge, surrounded with such characteristic statements as the following: "all were involved in an original experience, an experience so original that nothing in the past experience of anyone was a preparation enabling one to recognize the new experience . . ."; and "he was his own colossol fortune." They do not belong to our dualistic, fragmented world. Schwartz "worships" them. And why not? They help him believe that they—and he—can achieve Transcendence.

Isaac Rosenfeld could not accept orthodox religion: "the cost of this religious importation is too great; we must pay for it in the dying out of the sense of life; in a doom of submission to a world ruled by dead men who, because they can no longer feel love, can no longer feel anything." Nor could he completely accept Philosophical Naturalism: it acknowledges "the need for moral security, for belief" only as "a deviation from an arbitrary standard of rational behavior." *The sense of life is Transcendent.* But in our "age of enormity"—to use his phrase—this sense is easily defeated by institutionalized belief, habit, or anxiety. The concentration camps, new "model reality," symbolize this victory. "The death of our old culture came about when the evil greater than the evil occurred—which is the terror." [8] How to recapture the sense of life? How to find "joy, which wants eternity?" These questions troubled Rosenfeld and compelled him to search everywhere.

Passage from Home represents an early phase of his search. Bernard, the adolescent hero, cannot believe in Judaism—it has not really given joy to his tense father or *saved* him. When he drinks the Passover wine, he thinks that "this holiday . . . was something my family could not understand, a celebration not even of this earth, its meaning lying beyond the particular individual." Passover is Transcendent for Bernard not in its historical associations but in its sense of life. Throughout the novel he has similar visions: *doctrine as such is less meaningful than celebration.* Thus when he watches his step-mother clean the house on Friday, he calls this task a "religious ceremony" because it lifts her out of her daily routine and makes her whole (or holy). He admires Reb Feldman, the Hassid, who can even transform rude people when he sings about God. But Bernard asks gloomily, "Why were people incapable of remaining fixed to the best moments of their lives?"

In his last years Rosenfeld had to be certain that he would not lose Transcendence. He had to see It not as some kind of temporary glow but as part of a stable pattern. He sought Fixity—and found it in the "science-mysticism" of Wilhelm Reich.

Of course, it is easy to dismiss Reichian psychology as the product of madness. But as a "significant" substitute for religion, it influences Shapiro, Bellow, Paul Goodman, and Mailer; it sanely reaffirms, for them, the sense of life.[9] At the center of Reichian psychology is the concept of "orgone energy." This energy permeates the universe; when the individual is "in tune" with it—worshipping it in his own orgasmic flow—he is transformed. Healthy sex unites the human and the cosmic, body and energy, creating "cosmic consciousness." Here is Karl Shapiro discussing Reich in *In Defense of Ignorance*.

The basis for the hatred of Reich is, of course, his use of sex therapy and his theory of the orgasm, which were as offensive to psychological "science" as to the police and the clergy. Reich nevertheless speaks to the poet and the mystic as well as to the scientist. The feeling of having one's roots in nature, he says, is common to all great poets and writers, thinkers and artists, just as it is always felt in true religion though never completely realized. And because this sense of being rooted in nature either has been experienced mystically or attributed to the eternally unknowable regions beyond human ken, the search for knowledge, according to Reich, has always turned into superstitious, irrational, metaphysical beliefs.

. . . .

To the poet and mystic it will be evident that what Reich calls the cosmic-energy ocean in which all things exist is indeed what others call God.

Rosenfeld's last stories are steeped in Reichian Transcendence. "George," which appeared in *Partisan Review* (July–August, 1952), is one of these. George opens the story by remarking to the narrator that he is bored by "bodies"—he wants only to be "a pure intelligence"—and he promptly walks out of the window. He doesn't fall; he "settles" to the ground like a leaf—"incredibly light!" The narrator then explains the events which led to this odd departure. At a party without much character—a "diseased" one—everyone was having a good time, not communicating. George arrived and immediately understood that the guests were afraid of their own being; they did not submit to the sense of life. George was offended by this "frantic, dirty spirit, this misery they were all so full of that night." Foolish Gloria undressed, out of spite, and the men ogled her body. At this point he departed. Why should the narrator (and Rosenfeld) spend so much time on such a "trivial" incident? George emerges as a neurotic "saint" because he sees the division of personality—the dirtiness of flirting. He demonstrates, through his departure, that he can rise above things— that, in a sense, he is full of cosmic energy. He reminds us of Rosenfeld's journal entry, "To know, to know, to know . . . knowledge and love combined into the one ecstasy, the highest good of mind and body."

"In the Holy City" appeared in *New World Writing 20*. Pathfinder spends time in the monastery. Here he finds that he "could not make a step without becoming aware of his brutishness." The monks resemble George; they move "musically"; they live with their bodies. Ko-Han, one of them, delicately eats spiders to lower himself before his God. These mad adventures continue in the city itself. When Pathfinder leaves the monastery, he sees that "wild animals are allowed to roam in the streets." The citizens do not fear them. They live peacefully with them. He gazes at naked women in the forest who lack shame; one winks at him. "Never had flesh so surprised him, never surprised him at all." Now for the first time Pathfinder skips along full of "joy and energy"; "he had a sense of his life, mere life, living itself out in a long, continuous, neglected sweep, unknown, under water." And after he visits The Thing, the high priest, he learns that the Enemy still lies in himself. Why does Rosenfeld contrast the joy to the terror of self? He apparently believes that before Pathfinder can become "saintly," he must purge his internal enemy which prevents him from enjoying the full sense of life. Nevertheless, his new hero, like George, is "on the way," affirming Transcendence even in spiders. He must continue to "work" to find Joy.

Leslie Fiedler cannot relinquish dualities, as Rosenfeld did, for one System of Transcendence. In his lastest book of criticism, *No! in Thunder*, he still believes that the writer must exile himself from perfect liberal dreams, that personality as such is "radically imperfect." But he affirms, at the same time, "having endured a vision of the meaninglessness of existence, [such a writer] retreats neither into self-pity and aggrieved silence nor into a realm of beautiful lies. He chooses, rather, to render the absurdity which he perceives, to know it and make it known. To know and to render, however, means to give form; and to give form is to provide the possibility of delight—a delight which does not deny horror but lives at its intolerable heart."

Fiedler finds Transcendence in archetypal thinking. In "Archetype and Signature" he deals with the "relationship of poet and poem," attacking those critics who slight this relationship. The "reductive" approach which maintains that the poem is the poet (that "the work of art [is] *nothing but* the personality of the Genius behind it"); the "intrinsic" approach which maintains that the poem exists without the poet— both approaches do not comprehend artistic unity. "Poetry" is Transcendent because it heals incoherence or polarization; it marries language and personality, enriching poet and reader. But this is only the first step. Poetry also marries signature and archetype. "I use 'Signature' to mean the sum total of individuating factors in a work, the sign of the Persona or Personality through which an Archetype is rendered, and which itself tends to become a subject as well as a means of the poem." Archetype means "any of the immemorial patterns of response to the human situation in its most permanent aspects: death, love, the biological family, the relationship with the Unknown, etc." Poetry achieves Transcendence for Fiedler because it embodies *the personal recognition of eternal patterns:* The inferior poet—or the incomplete person—can only do justice to one of the terms, projecting his personality into a void, *or* destroying it; the great poet sees himself in relation to some Higher Being—the Archetype. By responding to this work, the reader marries the poet. "A final way back into the world of the Archetypes, available even in our atomized culture, is an extension of the way instinctively sought by the Romantics, down through the personality of the poet, past his particular foibles and eccentricities, to his unconscious core, where he becomes one with us all in the presence of our ancient Gods."

Fiedler's theory (which supplies the rationale for his concern with Kafka as Mythic Jew, the Faustian Archetype in American fiction etc.) is related to the Reichianism of Rosenfeld and the cosmic consciousness of Karl Shapiro. It is also a new faith which attempts to rise above dualities. It *cares* about the healthy union of opposites, suggesting that Joy results from exposure to Wholeness.

In a recent essay (published in *Ramparts*, Fall, 1963), Fiedler directs his attention to "The Jew as Mythic American." Jewishness, for him, is more than doctrine; it is an archetypal pattern of response. He agrees with the present author that a Leon Uris or Harry Golden is not in touch with such experience. For Fiedler the archetype must be defined (or redefined) after it has been tarnished by commercial signatures; it must be "reclaimed." He tells us: "the compelling images of Jews were made by writers who were not merely Gentiles but anti-Semites, interested in resisting this assimilationist impulse, and keeping the Jews Jews." He admires Hemingway's Robert Cohn and Nathaniel West's Jews because they are more Jewish—less stereotyped—than Uris' Jews. Our new writers—the writers I have been discussing—must, according to Fielder, resist the artificial images of the crowd and purify the archetype. Underneath these sophisticated, rebellious theories lies a simple desire: the wholeness of Jewish identity—of human identity—must be reasserted. Fiedler is, like his fellow writers, a prophet of Transcendence. His God may not be an official one, but He does follow the spirit, if not the law.

Fiedler suggests in the same essay that Saul Bellow (and Norman Mailer) has moved from the "mythical Jew established in the literature of the forties and the fifties: the alienated intellectual, uneasily at home only in the world of culture . . . to imagine [himself] as mythical [Gentile]:   paleface Protestant Noble Savage." It is true that the "dangling man" or "victim" has been replaced by the "rain king." But is Bellow completely surrendering his Jewishness? I don't think so. *Henderson the Rain King* and "The Wrecker" resemble Rosenfeld's "George"; all three are infused with Hasidic joy—the union of body and soul. Wilhelm Reich is, after all, a "brother" to the great Hasidic Masters who, at times, lost themselves in a cosmic dance which shocked their more orthodox co-religionists. Are these statements about Joy Hasidic or Reichian? "No child can be born except through pleasure and joy." "If we are habitually joyful, we shall be released from every tribulation." Both are Hasidic but they could easily be inserted into Reichian psychology (if not style) or *Henderson the Rain King*. Theodore Solotaroff's discussion of Rosenfeld's Reichianism applies as well to Bellow's recent fiction.

> Naturalist that he was, Rosenfeld saw the way out of the underground not through Jewish faith in another redemptive place, but through the satisfaction of his natural desires. But he was a mystic for all that—and a Jewish one. He tried to bridge the gap between alienation and connection, depression and joy, secular-

ism and transcendence, through the flesh rather than through religious experience, and he found his mentor in Wilhelm Reich. However, Rosenfeld's Reichianism, under the inevitable conditioning of his character, often reads as much like Hasidism. "To love all love," he writes at one point in his journal, "even the beloved partner's love for another. For then we see the world spelled out in letters of flame." [9]

Let us look closely at *Henderson the Rain King*. Here the search for Transcendence strikes through the mask of dualities, especially those of body and spirit, intellect and feeling. Joy is found in eternal "becoming."

In Africa Henderson discovers at first that if one looks properly, he can see reality under appearance— indeed there is no significant difference between the two. *The body is always true.* Queen Willatale informs him that he has a great "capacity" for life, indicated by [his] largeness, and especially [his] nose." Henderson kisses her middle, finding the embrace a "significant experience." This unity of body and soul is also suggested by the spiritualization of things: object-world holds spirit-world. Thus Henderson claims that he hears the "voices of objects and colors"; he loses himself (and finds himself) in "practical tasks." He "tricks" life by disregarding dualities.

Dahfu joins Henderson in dialogues about truth. The same ideas are stressed as before, but they are more "substantial." When Henderson encounters the ruler of the Wairiris, he believes that his previous insights have not yet captured truth. He is assailed by many doubts. Dahfu hints at his "unrest," although his body seems at ease. He is pleasant but he is savage. Henderson thinks, "But my purpose was to see essentials, only essentials, nothing but essentials, and to guard against hallucinations. Things are not what they seem anyway." Dahfu may be a "con-man." The savage ruler offers advice. "The world of facts is real, all right, and not to be altered. The physical is all there, and it belongs to science. But then there is the noumenal department, and there we create and create and create." The imagination, he instructs Henderson, can see truth everywhere. But it can also create lies. There is thus no easy solution to masquerades. *They are within us at all times.* But this fact is not "hopeless." Henderson sees that reality is never grasped without hallucinations. One term presupposes the other. *Becoming is the Transcendence of both terms.*

Dahfu continues, "Men of most powerful appetite have always been the ones to doubt reality the most." Henderson acknowledges the truth of this remark, largely because he is more overwhelmed by Dahfu's tales of the lion-father he—as ruler—must capture. Is Dahfu real? he asks. His question plagues him, especially after his dark teacher says, Man "is the master of adaptations. He is the artist of suggestions." (We have come a long way from the masquerades of *The Victim.* Bellow seems here to be saying that masquerades exalt *and* debase us.) The body-spirit unity which was implied earlier is reemphasized. Dahfu says, "Disease is a speech of the psyche." According to this aphorism, tics reveal inner disturbance; missing teeth reveal missing knowledge and so on. Such occult knowledge makes Henderson act like a lion—if he can *roar,* he can be brave! So he is "the beast," assuming the voice and gestures of the lion. Dahfu even partially convinces Henderson that "inanimate objects might have a mental existence." But our "rain king" still doubts the truth of this astounding remark. (Dahfu has probably read Wilhelm Reich. Reich insists—as do the Hasidic Masters—that body and soul are one. The body reveals inner tensions. Here are some typical remarks by Reich: "*Emotion is an expressive plas-matic motion.*" [10] "*We work with the expressive lan-guage*. Only when we have *felt* the facial *expression* of the patient are we also in a position to understand it.*" [11] It is interesting to note that both Reich and Dahfu—who claim that there are no appearances, *merely realities*—are regarded as "con-men," who fur-ther their *own* truth by masquerade.)

To return to Henderson. He learns, after these "conflicting truths," that reality is never grasped. The lion Dahfu and he assume is the old king, turns out to be another "person." It kills Dahfu. Hypocrisy is very close to Henderson—the consorts desire his life when *he* becomes king. We consider Henderson's flight from Africa—before they kill him—as another attempt to find truth, despite "the bad stuff . . . coming back." There is no pure truth—without mas-querade—as there are not eternal courts of heaven. Becoming doesn't cease—it is always "leaping, leap-ing, pounding, and tingling." But in this tingling lies momentary Joy.

Miracle, magic, and coincidence—why do these "occult" phenomena occur so frequently in Bernard Malamud's stories? Although they are not viewed as divinely given, they function as symbols of "unnatu-ral" power which interferes with human activity. They are Transcendent.

"Angel Levine" is, on the surface, a humorous tale. Manischevitz, a tailor who "suffered many reverses and indignities," prays to God that things should improve—after all, why should only evil happen to *him?* One day he sees a Negro named Levine, who is not only a Jew but an angel! Manischevitz believes that the Negro is unreal, but after a while, he searches for him, hoping but not believing that he will work a miracle and make him (and his wife) better. Malamud does not take the matter "seriously"; perhaps he is interested only in the punch line—"there are Jews everywhere." But by granting Levine angelic power (which *is* effective), he implies that there is some Force which gives Manischevitz "a new life." What is this Force? Is it *God?* Is it *luck?* Is it *faith?*

Once we ask these questions (and reread the story), we realize that Manischevitz is a non-believer. He prays to God only when he needs Him. His religion— not a matter of doctrines—is invoked *occasionally.* "Manischevitz visited a synagogue and there spoke to God but God had absented himself. The tailor searched his heart and found no hope. . . . He railed against God—Can you love a rock, a broom, an emptiness? Baring his chest, he smote the naked bones, cursing himself for having believed." Even non-believers, however, see signs. Malamud does not believe in signs from the God of his ancestors. The signs which Manischevitz sees later are "funny" and heretical but, ironically enough, they affirm that life is hopeful, changeable, and in this sense, miraculous. Malamud believes in "miracles" but not Judaism.

Thus he lives in some half-way house. He has moved from orthodoxy, but he has not substituted a new religion for it. He is still fascinated by the other world—whether he labels it fantastic luck, chance, or faith. His stories are filled with symbols of this half-way position. They contain the ghetto and the sky. The ghetto is the daily routine, the life without joy or faith—it appears as the stores owned by Feld ("The First Seven Years"), Morris Bober, and Tommy Castelli ("The Prison"); the rooms occupied by Kessler ("The Mourners"), Finkle ("The Magic Barrel") and "The German Refugee." The sky—or "pastoral" nature—is where extraordinary events occur; it is the setting for new (or Transcendent) life. Finkle rushes forward to kiss Stella: "violins and lit candles revolved in the sky." (Stella is his Joy, although she is Salzman's Terror.) Levine is "borne aloft on a pair of magnificent black wings." Mitka dreams of waltzing "around his writing chamber" with Mrs. Lutz. Isaac, the idiot, travels to California. This contrast between the ghetto and the sky—between earthly dualism and Transcendence—demonstrates that Malamud has not "left the ground," but he still continues to see magic there.

And Philip Roth? Does he believe in Transcendence? He apparently does in "Eli, the Fanatic" and "The Conversion of the Jews." Both Eli Peck and Ozzie Friedman, upset by dualities, transcend them in visions of holiness. But their visions are rather "free." This is the problem: we feel that Eli and Ozzie are unbalanced, that they are hallucinating. Transcendence is tinged with "madness" (as it is in *Henderson the Rain King*). Consequently, it remains private, not encompassing the universe. When Roth tells us in "Eli, the Fanatic" that "the drug calmed his soul, but did not touch it down where the blackness had reached . . . we are unsure about the source of that blackness. Does it come from Eli's madness or from some Higher Force? And Ozzie's fall "into the center, of the yellow net that glowed in the evening's edge like an overgrown halo"? Has he seen God or his own rebellious pride?

The same problem arises in *Letting Go.* Paul Herz returns to Brooklyn after his father's death. In the cemetery he examines the faces of his relatives—the black hair of his cousin Clare, his Aunt Gertie's mouth. Suddenly he sees the meaning as he kisses Mother.

> He kissed nothing—only held out his arms, open, and stood still at last, momentarily at rest in the center of the storm through which he had been traveling all these

years. For his truth was revealed to him, his final premise melted away. What he had taken for order was chaos. Justice was illusion.

But the meaning is unclear (as it is for Ozzie and Eli). Paul sees the chaos of his previous actions, thereby affirming some standard of order. Where is that order? How does it function? We don't know. Later in the novel he adopts some kind of Jewish way of life: Libby, his wife, even lights the Sabbath candles. This conversion is again too inexplicable to be true. Thus like their "brothers"—the narrator of "The Tingling Back," Manischevitz, Pathfinder etc.—Roth's "mad crusaders" are converts—they have given up traditional Jewish doctrines, substituting for them some kind of new faith. But this faith seems unnatural, tricky, or "private."

This is not to claim that our writers are phony; they sincerely want to transcend the dualities which plague them, but they are afraid to embrace "orthodoxy." It is ironic that their definitions of Transcendence are, at times, as "rigid" and "self-deceiving" as the Judaism *they* fear. They are back at the beginning. They have faced traditional dualities and transcended them, if only momentarily, affirming universal order. Now they feel "less Jewish." But their conversion is somewhat unreal. And with their new insights and errors—which aren't new at all—they are still preoccupied with their heritage. They cannot "let go."

7 IRONY

OUR WRITERS use traditional devices to present their quest for God: "Jewish irony," fantasy, and parable.

In a recent article on "The Traditional Roots of Jewish Humor," Israel Knox maintains that this humor can be categorized in three ways: as irony, "tragic optimism," and the "intermingling of 'Is' and 'Ought.'" [1] "The Talmud is wary of jesting except at idolatry, and it is this kind of 'jesting,' this strain of irony, that has been the constant element in Jewish laughter from Elijah the prophet to Sholem Aleichem's Tevye." [2] Irony expresses the "will toward righteousness": "so long as the actual and the ideal are disparate, so long as the hopes of the heart are not embodied in the contexture of things about us, there is work for man to do, and there is the urgency to stir the conscious to do the work. . . . The world is moving toward the Messianic fulfillment, but the 'future comes one day at a time.'" [3] Mr. Knox's categories overlap, of course, but the striking thing about his analysis is that it affirms the "dualistic thinking" of Jewish tradition. This tradition, as we have seen, demands polarization—Exile and Land, Head and Heart etc.—and it turns often to irony, rather than farce or slap-stick, to express such polarization. Even "renegade" Jews never surrender their irony. Although

Franz Kafka, for example, did not accept orthodox Judaism, he still viewed life in a "traditional" way. (Thomas Mann calls him a "religious humorist.") One of his parables contains the essence of the ironic intermingling of actual and ideal; it confirms Mr. Knox's brilliant analysis. "Leopards break into the temple and drink to the dregs what is in the sacrificial pitchers; this is repeated over and over again; finally it can be calculated in advance, and it becomes a part of the ceremony." [4]

Let us turn to our seven writers. I will concentrate on two or three examples of Jewish irony in their work, hoping that these are representative.

In his introduction to *Poems of a Jew* Karl Shapiro writes that he "grew up in an atmosphere of mysterious pride and sensitivity, an atmosphere in which even the greatest achievement was touched by a sense of the comic." (Another intermingling of actual and ideal, "low and high.") In his best work he retains this "sense of the comic," not surrendering it to some Transcendent Feeling. "Teasing the Nuns" seems a rather simple poem. It deals with "the Jew's inability to speak to the nuns." But the poem develops "cosmic" intermingling by means of its complex, "funny" imagery. In the first stanza (there are only two) we see the nuns in the elevator; they are going up. "Up" denotes the top floor in the building, but it also suggests heaven, closeness to God. The nuns, married to Christ, are divorced from Him; they must live on earth—even ride elevators! They are likened to "undomestic ducks," "gay in captivity." These similes are witty—nuns aren't usually considered "wild" or "twittery"—they suggest again that the soul is uncomfortable in its new home; it is not domesticated to earthly existence. Then the narrator says "we"; he is in this fast-moving elevator, "Yanked into heaven by a hairy

Roc." There is something "fabulous," "eternal," about the mundane; "Sinbad" lives today. The next few lines describe their exodus from the elevator (or cage): the nuns and the narrator emerge in a "towery cell." The cell is a classroom; the nuns are students; the narrator is the teacher. Everything is topsy-turvy. The nuns *should* pray; they *should* not be college "freshmen"; and the narrator *should* be more concerned with his own poetry, if not salvation. Now we understand the imagistic insistence on animals (which continues in this part of the poem: the nuns have "elegant bird-names"): *humanity is not adjusted to its role; it is actual and ideal and, therefore, comic.* The narrator proceeds in the next stanza—which contains one line—to speak; perhaps he will comment on the "human predicament" or the "human comedy." He murmurs one word, "sisters," and stops. (Does he mean that he is their "brother" in exile?) The poem ends with silence. One question remains: Why has Shapiro used his title? *Who* teases the nuns? What does he do? Of course, we can say that the narrator teases the sisters by calling them "ducks" etc. Maybe the humor is deeper. The world of actuality teases the world of potentiality; we are not what we seem.

"The Convert" is another comic poem. Shapiro uses irony "as a way of telling the truth, of putting matters right, of extending a partial perspective into a more comprehensive one, of letting light in where there was half-darkness." [5] He attacks the "idolatry" of conversion. The entire poem is filled with irony, but the third stanza is perhaps the most dramatic. Shapiro believes that the convert violates his past neutrality (and humanity) by adhering rigidly to the Book: "Yet he shall be less perfect than before, / Being no longer neutral to the Book / But answerable." The convert, in seeking perfection, achieves radical imperfection. Before he read the Book, he viewed Life itself as a "natural" work; now It is Official Doctrine or what Shapiro calls "official news." And in the rest of the stanza, the convert is pictured ironically as automatic: "The dust of ages settles on his mind / And in his ears he hears the click of beads / Adding, adding, adding like a prayer machine / His heartfelt sums." The beads are handled without wonder; they are clicked like a typewriter or some religious adding machine. The convert becomes an accountant! Shapiro is using irony to assert "righteousness"; he knows that even the best intentions—conversion and salvation—are easily seduced by the rigid intellect. Again he sees the ideal corrupted by the actual, and he smiles bitterly.

Heinz Politzer has written that "the incompatibility of experience and consciousness—the contradiction between the banality and ugliness of daily life and the truth and beauty of intellectual existence—has remained ever present to [Delmore] Schwartz." [6] We would expect Schwartz to use irony to capture this incompatibility; he is, after all, "an inconoclast out of love for the pure image." [7] (Only when he finds the pure image in his later work does he lose righteous irony.)

In a section entitled "Pleasure" from the long poem "Coriolanus and His Mother," Schwartz steps onto the stage. He proclaims that he "knows very few witty sayings, entertaining stories." But he tries to make the audience laugh, quoting Stendhal's remarks about ice-cream: "What a pity it is not a sin." Then he becomes more serious, maintaining that pleasure is born out of pain, that humor arises from incompatibility: "we . . . know that we cannot regard the warm identity beneath our faces as being no more than an abstraction." Presumably we must do something to confirm our individuality. But what? We have our pleasures. Schwartz ticks them off ironically, trying to show that because most pleasure disregards the underlying pain of life, it is shallow. "Pleasure of having a child (O my son Absalom, graduating from high school!)." Note the contrast between high and low, Absalom and the average teenager. "The pleasure of ritual, the gloves drawn on precisely." Dressing is as pleasurable as religious ritual. And so on. Schwartz' "epic catalogue" debases our daily pleasures; it asks us to define them clearly. "Let us, I say, make a few sharp clear definite observations before we die." Humor is "entertaining," to return to his opening remarks, because it helps us stare at ourselves—our secret longings, our dissipated pleasures—with "strength and power." It is bitterly pleasurable.

Schwartz uses irony in his early poems. "The Heavy Bear Who Goes With Me" is representative. The first stanza describes this bear, using appropriate "natural" imagery. "He" is "clumsy and lumbering"; he is in love with "candy, anger, and sleep," and he displays his strength by climbing buildings or kicking footballs. Of course, the description is "precise" but it is more: the bear is "unreal": he symbolizes the body, the grossness of humanity. Although he is friendly in the first few lines, he soon gets out of hand. He becomes a "crazy factotum," ruling his "master." The second stanza develops this victory. The bear won't let his master—the soul or enlightened consciousness—rest at all; he howls for sweetness, a "world of sugar." And he is "terrified, / Dressed in his dress-suit, . . . "; he trembles to think of his own cut-up meat. In the third stanza he is "inescapable"—a "stupid clown," a "caricature" who distorts the spirit's "motive" and "gesture." He drags his master everywhere, finally showing him the "hundred million of his kind, / The scrimmage of appetite everywhere." These last two lines are especially forceful because they show us the bear as only *one* of an entire family. Funny? Entertaining? Of course not. Schwartz' humor rages at existence; it is born out of a sense of righteousness which demands (of God?) less monstrous humanity, more perfection.

In an essay on Sholem Aleichem, Isaac Rosenfeld deals with the "humor of exile." (The phrase captures the essence of Jewish humor.) Aleichem, we are told, "constructed a comedy of endurance, balancing the fantastic excess of misfortune (always short of life's complete destruction, yet always threatening to attain its end) against the precious but useless resources of the human spirit which can make equally fantastic accommodations, can even overwhelm the world with its enthusiasm, and yet remains no less impotent than the despair it sedulously avoids." Isn't this comedy of endurance necessarily ironic, intermingling as it does the actual (misfortune, destruction, the "bear") and the ideal (happiness or perfection)? Irony, to quote Rosenfeld, often brings together "the patient and the author of suffering."

"King Solomon," one of Rosenfeld's last stories, is filled with Jewish humor (as is "The Hand That Fed Me," *Passage from Home*, etc.). We meet a Solomon who is not an ideal patriarch—a superhuman figure— but a suffering old man; and the ironic contrasts involved make us see the continuity of history—of misfortune. The first section, "With His Women," introduces us to "charismatic" Solomon; his counselors don't understand his wonderful ways with women. "None has seen the King's nakedness; yet all have seen him in shirt sleeves or suspenders, paunchy, loose-jowled, in need of a trim." (Some nobility!) Because Rosenfeld humanizes him, we smile at the fact that he resembles, if only partially, one of us. We recognize his bunions, his jowls, his sadness. But we mourn his lost divinity—there are no miracles left! The third section, "With His Fathers," shows us an even lower Solomon (after the visit of the Queen of Sheba): "he warms his hands on the water bottle, presses it to his cheek, passes it down along his belly." He muses about his past: Who made him king? What was the glory of the king? The questions remain unanswered (and unanswerable). Solomon, like any other man, "knows only that once love was with him, which now is no more." Our identification with him is no longer "humorous"; it is extremely unpleasant.

In one parable Rosenfeld is even more "outraged" at our lot. A soldier has a horse; "the two of them were friends and confided in each other, though the horse hadn't the power of speech." This ideal situation, so unlike the one in Schwartz' "Heavy Bear," cannot last. One day the soldier suggests to the horse that a girl, Zelda, loves him, and the horse, wondering about the nature of love, *courts* her. He knocks on her door; she doesn't open it. He runs away. He begins to brood. "Am I to blame that I'm a horse? But how can I remain content with being a horse?" Later he and his master meet Zelda on the road; he is so upset that he falls and breaks his leg; and he waits eagerly to be shot. Why is the parable funny? Is it because the animal and human are reversed (as, interestingly enough, it is in "Teasing the Nuns" and "The Heavy Bear Who Goes with Me")? We don't expect horses to *think*— let alone to fall in love with girls. But underlying this rather easy reversal is a deeper cause of humor: the horse is exiled from some ideal picture of himself, divorced from full realization of his potentialities. He does not realize or accept his *horseness*. Suffering *and* enthusiatic—he resembles Sholom Aleichem's Tevye. Rosenfeld's parable, like "King Solomon," begins in laughter at the inversion of roles, the topsy-turvy world, and ends in painful knowledge of "divided" humanity. But let Rosenfeld himself comment on the parable. The horse wants "freedom greater than it is his nature to exercise. . . . This very discovery discloses to him that he is not free." Here is the problem.

> Here cuts the double edge of freedom with its terrible, excellent sharpness: one edge toward ourselves—how sharp the limit is!—and the other, more terrible, away from us—what a deep cut we have taken of the impossible! Sheathe either edge and you are defeated. Without the wound of the limit, you would cut without blood; it is idealism, in the disgraceful sense, to believe in a freedom without limit, it is unreality and cowardice. Sheathe the outer edge and you have a worse cowardice, called determinism, but actually, contentment with things as they are, smugness, the amoral convent. Sheathe both edges and you have dullness on your hands.

Leslie Fiedler also uses humor to "pull down vanity." *The Second Stone* attacks idolatrous Love. Although Mark Stone is the spiritual leader of the First International Congress on Love, he knows nothing about the subject. He can quote Buber (who doesn't attend the Congress), Andreas Capellanus, and Plato; he can admire Zen, Judaism, and Existentialism—these surface allegiances hide the simple fact that he is impotent. The estrangement of Mark's impotence (or indifference) from his "ideal" statements is so great that we smile bitterly. There are many ironic juxtapositions in the novel: Hilda, Mark's wife, falls in love with Clem; a musing listener at the Congress masturbates; Mark's patron manufactures, of all things, contraceptives. But these are perhaps less effective than the farewell dinner. Mark spouts Wisdom about the "divinity implicit in the created world," which he has not accepted in his own marriage. As the various participants speak about Love, they reveal that they cannot even communicate to — let alone love — each other. "Christianity minus Grace," Andy Gump, Jean Harlow, and Biblical Hebrew — there is a riot of violent contrasts. At last Mark is urged by his disciples — the dinner is a pseudo-Last Supper — to repeat his thoughts about Love. He does (against Hilda's objections): *"There is an old saying of our People that until a man has taken to his bosom the Shekhinah Below, i.e., a wife, there will not descend. . . ."* Hilda screams: How do you dare?" They fight. Mark beats his wife with a "rolled-up copy of *Thou*, unable to stop stuttering, 'I—I—I—I—.'" Fiedler's irony doesn't cease here. He makes us see that Hilda and Clem, who return to their respective partners, do rise above the petty, self-centered motives of Mark, the false Messiah; they do love each other, knowing that, unfortunately, it is better not to live together. This "love story" ends with Mark striking Hilda (the world itself); Clem, the true lover, barks "like a fox," accepting the beastliness of love.

Because Fiedler recognizes that the serious writer must "confess . . . the inevitable discrepancy between dream and fact, between the best man can imagine and the best he can achieve," he uses irony to tell the truth, "accepting the tragic implications of that truth, the vision of an eternal gap between imagined order and actual chaos." His critical essays are filled with savage irony. On sterile young critics: "Each does what he can; and construing a poem by John Crowe Ransom, though it may not be as good as writing it, is considerably better than biting your fingernails" ("The Un-Angry Young Man"). On the "modishness" of Jewish-American literature: "It is, indeed, [the Jews'], quite justified claim to have been *first* to occupy the Lost Desert at the center of the Great American Oasis (toward which every one now races Coca-Cola in one hand, Martin Buber in the other)" ("The Jew as Mythic American"). On scholarly studies of the twenties: "The only real blasphemy still possible to us is to write a history of blasphemies between the Great War and the Great Depression in which we prove those blasphemies merely manifestations of a deeper piety than ours" ("The Ant on the Grasshopper"). But these ironies are part of more significant ones: In America "togetherness" is incestuous; freedom is obsessive domination; national enlightenment is diabolism. (Such ironies abound in *Love and Death in the American Novel*.) Fiedler's criticism is, then, saying *No! in Thunder*. It is as humorous as Rosenfeld's fables or Schwartz' "heavy bear," not only "lightening but enriching despair."

Saul Bellow also sees the "intermingling of 'Is' and 'Ought.'" His heroes are obsessed by dualities; they walk the line between dream and fact, laughing at their precarious position. They are Jewish ironists.

Dangling Man is, to quote Joseph, a "bureaucratic comedy." He laughs at his position in a dark way, realizing how "funny" things are: Here he is, a grown man, living in his room, afraid to do anything! His wife supports him! Occasionally he rationalizes and claims "there is an element of the comic or fantastic in everyone. You can never bring that altogether under control." But he cannot rationalize successfully when he is confronted by the "Spirit of Alternatives," his alter ego; perhaps the most grimly comic incidents occur when the two converse.

"Then only one question remains."
"What?"
"Whether you have a separate destiny. Oh you're a shrewd wiggler," said *Tu As Raison Aussi*. "But I've

been waiting for you to cross my corner. Well, what do you say?"

I think I must have grown pale.

"I'm not ready to answer. I have nothing to say to that now."

"How seriously you take this," cried *Tu As Raison Aussi.*

"It's only a discussion. The boy's teeth are chattering. Do you have a chill?" He ran to get a blanket from the bed.

Joseph shrugs ironically, afraid to face his cosmic awkwardness. But his very solemnity—which tends to be "exaggerated"—mocks itself.

The Victim contains the same kind of irony. Because Asa and Allbee are fools, we have a "comedy of errors"; life is viewed as a series of mistakes, the intermingling of actuality and dream. Consider, for example, this conversation:

> "After the way you've acted I should throw you out. And if you really believe half the things you said to me, you shouldn't want to stay under the same roof. You're a lousy counterfeit."
>
> "Why you have the whole place to yourself. You can put me up," Allbee said smiling. "I wouldn't be inconveniencing you. But if you want me to do this in the right spirit . . ." And to Leventhal's astonishment—he was too confounded when it happened to utter a sound—Allbee sank out of his chair and went to his knees.
>
> Then he shouted, "Get up!"
>
> Allbee pulled himself to his feet.

The conversation is ironic: two weaklings—both dependent upon each other quarrel because they do not want to see themselves clearly. Allbee shrewdly exaggerates his dependence by begging; Asa likes to see his demon in this position, but he is uncomfortable.

Bellow knows more: in his "will toward righteousness," he asserts that despite their limitations, both men are human; they have the potentiality to rise above such foolishness. His ambivalence creates painful comedy.

Augie March uses irony to accept life. After gazing at all the absurdities of existence—including his own position—he understands the ultimate purpose of humor as Asa and Allbee cannot. "That's the *animal ridens* in me, the laughing creature, forever rising up. What's so laughable, that a Jacqueline, for instance, as hard used as that by rough forces, will still refuse to lead a disappointed life? Or is the laugh at nature— including eternity—that it thinks it can win over us and the power of hope?" The laughing creature! How simple to say and hard to embrace! Augie's ability to laugh saves him. He rises above possible self-indulgence and sees that he is silly—a victim—but this very perception ennobles him. *Irony, then, is an enigma because it transcends categories of pain or joy; it resolves ambivalence in a mysterious way.*

In his introduction to *Great Jewish Short Stories*, Bellow agrees with Augie. He tells us that in Jewish stories "laughter and trembling are so curiously mingled that it is not easy to determine the relations of the two. At times the laughter seems simply to restore the equilibrium of sanity; at times the figures of the story, or parable, appear to invite or encourage trembling with the secret aim of overcoming it by means of laughter." Surely these comments apply not only to the stories Bellow includes in this anthology but to his own work.

"Laughter and trembling, the intermingling of 'Is' and 'Ought' "—such ironic dualities appear in Bernard Malamud's fiction. Every story in *The Magic Barrel* contains them: an ugly refugee works for many years in a shoe store because he loves the owner's daughter, but he doesn't reveal this love; a rabbinical student loves a whore; the pure, dreamlike heroine is a survivor of Nazi concentration camps; a "shady" Negro works "Jewish" miracles. And so on. Perhaps the most detailed ironies are found in *The Assistant*; I want to read it as a comedy.

The first page establishes the tone. Morris Bober arrives early in the morning to open the store for the Polish woman, who buys one unseeded roll. She is not grateful; she tells him that he is late. This small irony introduces larger ones. Morris has worked "seven days a week, sixteen hours a day," and he is close to bankruptcy. He is the most unlikely store-owner to be robbed; yet two thieves choose his dismal store. "It was his luck, others had better." Not only is goodness unrewarded; it is cast into the dirt. Malamud's irony expresses a "will toward righteousness" and it now turns "favorably." The criminal, Frank Alpine, is "sorry"; he returns to the "scene of the crime" and wants to help Morris. But he steals petty cash from the register! And the grocer protects him! The mixture of pleasure in misery, which is certainly here, is perhaps strongest when Frank spies on Helen Bober. Knowing that he will suffer if he takes advantage of her nudity—if he does evil—he goes ahead and stares at her in the shower. He is pained by her nakedness, which seems to reveal youthful beauty *and* loneliness. Longing is mingled with "mourning": "But in looking he was forcing her out of reach, making her into a thing only of his seeing, her eyes reflecting his sins, rotten past, spoiled ideals, his passion poisoned by his shame." Thus life continues ironically. Frank dislikes the Jews—"they got on his nerves"—but he wants to know more about them. He cannot tolerate their suffering; *he* resembles them in his suffering. Helen, who desires possibilities, falls in love with this past-dominated, unsuccessful Gentile. Two lines from their conversation captures their lives: "Life renews itself" and "My luck stays the same." When Frank sees his old friend, Ward Minogue, attack Helen, he rushes to her and saves her—and then attacks her. How ironic! But more so is that his earlier remark redeems him even now. "Even when I am bad I am good."

In the last third of the novel irony fully asserts itself as "tragic optimism"—to use Israel Knox's category. Because the world is "absurd"—as demonstrated by these inversions of goodness—it can equally destroy evil. It is comic, in other words, to see "victorious" evil defeated. Morris dies but is reborn in Frank Alpine; this "uncircumcised dog" becomes a Jew. But these surprising acts of goodness cannot *change the world*; they are, after all, only little gestures. The novel ends with these lines: "One day in April Frank went to the hospital and had himself circumcised. For a couple of days he dragged himself around with a pain between his legs. The pain enraged and inspired him. After Passover he became a Jew." The pain enraged and inspired him—in the juxtaposition of rage and inspiration lies not only the secret of Frank's conversion but the liberating (?) quality of Jewish irony in the entire novel.

"Epstein," by Philip Roth, also deals with the rage and inspiration of pain; it is probably his most ironic work (more so than the smart-aleck *Goodbye, Columbus*). We see middle-aged Epstein in bed next to his wife, Goldie; it is Friday night and the *shabus* candles flicker downstairs. Roth is too enraged to give us stereotyped, ideal images. He ironically "debases" these: Epstein thinks not about the Sabbath but about Goldie's bellows-like behind. He then hears the unzipping and panting of the newly-arrived young people downstairs. Sabbath candles, "zipping and un-zipping, bodily decay, the longing for something bet-ter—these juxtapositions do not allow Epstein to rest; he moves between the actual and the ideal, perceiving (not as sharply as Roth) the crazy comedy of life. He does not think that he will be tinged—almost destroyed—by it. But one day he gives Ida Kaufman, his new neighbor, a lift. Kindness. Goodness. What do they lead to? He ends up *buying* her love—and "prickly heat"? This groin rash assumes symbolic value: it is, in effect, Epstein's very existence— mysterious, capricious, dirty, "innocent." When his daughter, Sheila, and Michael (the guest) fight with him, they use the rash to maintain that he is diseased. And his defense? He has none—except to cry that he still wants to *live:* "When they start taking things away from you, you reach out, you grab—maybe like a pig even, but you grab. And right, wrong, who knows! With tears in your eyes, who can even see the differ-ence!"

Epstein's whole world has been destroyed: accused of dirtiness, childish behavior, and betrayal by Goldie and the young people—cast out of the family!—he runs away. Later he is found, half-dead, in Ida Kauf-man's house. Now he is accepted; he can be pitied (if not loved) by Goldie and the others. The result of his mock-heroic rebellion? Although his "rash" can be cleaned up, Epstein is less healthy than before.

Israel Knox has written:

> If righteousness is the goal of history, as it is in the prophetic teaching, then there will be *estrangement* from the world as it is, and there will also be *involve-ment* in the world for what it may be if we will it. The estrangement and the involvement are correlative in the "long view," but in the routine of existence there

are complications, and the Jew who will jest with a mild irony: *Er vet kumen ven Moshiach vet kumen* will also intone the *Kaddish* prayer: "May He establish His kingdom during your life and during your days and during the life of all the house of Israel, even speedily and at a near time." [8]

Our writers use irony because they want the world to be better. Often their hostility (as they pull down vanity) is more striking than their desire for perfection, but this fact only emphasizes their dualistic thinking. Perhaps their irony is darker than that of their ancestors—after all, they can only see the Messiah as Wilhelm Reich or Martin Buber—but it possesses traditional roots. It still expresses deep "will toward righteousness."

CRITICS HAVE DISCUSSED the "urbanity" of our seven writers. Theodore Solotaroff, for example, believes that Rosenfeld's imagination is "typical of the literary temperament that he found in New York." [1] Sophistication, intellectualization, realism—these qualities come to mind when we think of Rosenfeld, Bellow, or Schwartz. But supporting their urbanity is a deep vein of fantasy.

Such fantasy has its traditional roots. In the definitive *Jewish Magic and Superstition* Joshua Trachtenberg tells us that,

> the Jewish people did not cease to live and grow when the New Testament was written. The two thousand years since have seen a steady expansion and development of its inner life. New religious concepts were advanced, the old were elaborated, and always the effort has been to make these something more than concepts, to weave them into the pattern of daily life, so that the Jew might live his religion. This was the sadly misunderstood "legalism" of Judaism. But alongside this formal development there was a constant elaboration of what we may call "folk religion"—ideas and practices that never met with the wholehearted approval of the religious leaders, but which enjoyed such wide popularity that they could not be altogether excluded from the field of religion. [2]

Folk-religion deals with Spirits of the Dead, magical procedure, amulets, astrology, and dreams. Trachtenberg's many examples indicate that Jewish tradition is suffused with what we would call "fantasy." Here are some examples: "If, on the way home from the ritual bath . . . 'a woman encounters a dog, her child will have an ugly dog-face, if she meets an ass, it will be stupid, if an ignorant lout, it will be an ignoramus.' " [3] "Eleazar of Worms offers these [interpretations of dreams]: 'if a man dreams he has a pain in one eye, a brother will fall ill; in both eyes, two brothers will be ill; if a tooth falls out, a son or some relative will die.' " [4] The fantastic element—call it dream, magic, or superstition—led the medieval Jew to God. "In the long pre-Freudian centuries, before the mystery of the dream was reduced to all too human terms, when men still listened for the voice of God in the still of the night, dreams [and all fantasy] played a greater role in shaping ideas and actions and careers than it is easy for us today to believe." [5]

Now the fantastic has lost its spiritual quality; it is only case history or science fiction. But our writers use fantasy—especially "bad" dreams—to capture another kind of life—a heightened, cosmic vision. Of course, they don't believe that God gives us prophetic dreams—they are too modern to accept such superstition. It is remarkable, nevertheless, how often they use fantasy to counterpoint urbanity, returning us to the dark, instinctual, childish foundations of spiritual quest. Fantasy, for them, still tells "the truth."

Thus our writers join one mainstream of American literature. (Again the Jew and the American meet.) Richard Chase has argued that the characteristic works of the American imagination have been romances, which describe "extreme ranges of experience," giving us "oddity, distortion of personality, dislocations of normal life." [6] Surely the Gothic tales of Poe, Hawthorne, and Henry James are related to *The Victim* or "Angel Levine." Leon Edel has written a brief introduction to a new edition of James' "ghostly tales" in which he informs us that "in the ghostly tale man is in touch with things beyond his senses—mysteries that go back to the fables of time." [7] Reading "The Jolly Corner," "William Wilson," and the Jewish-American works I will discuss in this chapter, we "can encounter the demoniacal" in the "comfortable daylight of our lives." [8] We can respond once more to awe-inspiring fantasy.

Although Karl Shapiro does not believe in orthodox Judaism (or folk-religion), he still deals with the fantastic. Underneath his realistic descriptions of urban life—of modern civilization—lie nameless terrors.

"The Dirty Word," deals, on one level, with a small boy's use of obscenity. The word, Shapiro tells us, "hops in the cage of the mind like the Pondicherry vulture, stomping with its heavy left claw on the sweet meat of the brain and tearing it with its vicious beak, ripping and chopping the flesh." It assumes harsh control. The boy cannot stop saying it or thinking about it. Now Shapiro enters the poem—he is the boy. He claims that although he has outlived the bird— obscenity no longer frightens and delights him?—he has "made pens to write these elegies" from its feathers. What does this deliberately mystifying prose-poem mean? Is it simply about dirty words? What is the Word? Perhaps we can answer these questions by viewing the poem as folk-religion. Trachtenberg tells us about the magical power of words—the medieval Jews believed in amulets and codes; they were afraid to *name* the Lord. [9] Shapiro is dealing with his Jewishness. He has violated the taboo; he has spoken the name—Jew or God—delighting in his "boyish" rebellion. But his delight threatens him. The "dirty word" is fantastic because, no matter how we interpret it, it assumes sacred control of the owner—the boy-poet who uses it.

"The Leg" concerns amputation. It begins in "twilight-sleep": the narrator "peers in the middle distance," trying to locate himself in relation not only to his missing leg but to life in general. He gazes at the ghostly nurse, the rubber hands, and the spooky room. Later he thinks about his leg (which is as "magical" as the dirty word), and he cries "as a child cries / Whose puppy is mangled under a screaming wheel." Finally he wakes up. He explores his stump, and he smiles because he need not obey a "surgical limb." The leg and the man—both "wonder" about each other: he must "cultivate the mind of the leg, / Pray for the part that is missing." He does. He tells the Father that the leg, the body itself, is only a sign that he is "senselessness and mud" in His palm. He asks for courage to walk again. In his notes to this strange poem Shapiro tells us that "in Freud's view, as in that of every Jew, multilation, circumcision, and 'the fear of being eaten' are all one." "The Leg" is a poem written during war and its subject is the wholeness even of the mutilated." Shapiro has used a realistic description (as he did in the previous poem), but he has made it fantastic by means of his imagery. The leg becomes a supernatural sign—demoniacal and angelic—it is no longer part of everyday life. It awakens in us fear of mutilation and desire for wholeness. When he uses the fantastic, as he does in both poems, Shapiro introduces the idea of Jewish castration. Although the amputee—the Jew without his God?—prays for forgiveness, he knows that more terrors await him. *This* world opens up; *the other world*, the destroying Father, takes him "angrily in hand."

Delamore Schwartz also uses fantasy in his poems, juxtaposing the other world of dreams and hallucinations to daily routine. This clash is responsible for many dramatic images. The sonnet "O City, City" begins with the phrase, "to live between terms." Schwartz' heroes live "between terms," suspended, as it were, between reality and superreality, the "average" and the visionary. In this sonnet the subway is where "death has his loud picture." Do we *hear* a picture? Is death in the *faces* of the commuters? Is he in their newspapers? Is death a commuter? Such fantastic questions are raised by this introductory image. Not only do the city dwellers live between terms; they ride with death, unaware that he is here and there. Schwartz continues seeing such otherness: the subway riders—during the rush hour—are among the "six million souls"; their breath is an "empty song." Claustrophobia, death, suspension—these introduce us to "unreality." So does accident. In the next few lines we see "the sliding auto's catastrophe," the "rising" office building. Machines—objects in general—threaten the safety of the entire population; their tyranny causes "anguished diminution." Such images are strengthened by the non-stop lines which race from "to live" to "we die." Now there is the pause in the sonnet. Schwartz rests "between terms." He tries to see another kind of vision; he prays for serenity. And when he resumes the sonnet, giving us the sestet, he asks, "Whence, if ever, shall come the actuality / Of a voice speaking the mind's knowing." He waits for a supernatural voice. He yearns for the "blisses of the commonplace"—to use Thomas Mann's phrase—"the white bed" should be neat again. Schwartz moves, therefore, from the subway and office building to the white bed—home? But all these places, no matter their urban location, are as fantastic as the loud picture of death.

Ghosts move throughout Schwartz' poems: he sees the "ghosts of James and Pierce in Harvard Yard" (who walk "between heaven and hell"); "Socrates' ghost"; Abraham and Orpheus; and in "Coriolanus" five ghosts in a "box-seat." Why are there so many ghosts? Schwartz uses apparitions—as does Henry James in "Sir Edward Orme" or "Turn of the Screw"—to reawaken in us the primitive belief in spirits. His ghosts are not mere hallucinations; they are as "real" as the demons and angels accepted by the medieval Jew. He discovers in them the fusion of fantasy and reality; they also live between terms. Three stanzas from "Prothalamion" demonstrate this discovery. Schwartz claims that his eyes are tired (from looking so much at his past), and he touches a chair, presses his face against the window, hoping to discover "The look of actuality, the certainty / Of those who run down stairs and drive a car." He longs for neatness—the white bed—to soothe his troubled eyes. But the familiar is alien. He imagines waking up next morning and seeing a lion, lamb, or "daemon breathing heavily." He is completely grotesque—a "circus self." In the last stanza Schwartz claims that he is an "octopus in love with God." (Notice the "absolute" fantasy here.) His mind is "deranged in swimming tubes," unable to see past "its own darkness." How can the octopus live out of its element? How can humanity see the other world? How can the "fantastic" be real?

Isaac Rosenfeld, discussing Kafka, writes, "His art is therefore a kind of realism, in the logical sense, in that it finds relationships to be objective. But what distinguishes his art from the animated philosophy that so many critics take it to be is that the objective relationships of the world are perceived in and evoked by things. The world, as in a mystical system, becomes a visible legend." This kind of realism informs "Coney Island Revisited." The amusement park, like Schwartz' subway, is realistically described: we see the barker sneering, the "mechanical dummy twitching its chest in laughter," and the excited crowds. But the description also invokes the fantastic so subtly that we accept the narrator's predicament (and location) as quite natural. When, for example, he remembers an "old fantasy" about the dummy, we go along with him. The fantasy involves "overtones of torture and sexual perversion [death by tickling; bare feet, armpits, private parts, finger, feather, velvet whip]." We accept his making love with Gladys in the underground fun-house while electric cars rush by. Therefore Coney Island becomes a "visible legend" in which a huge mechanical spider, dummy-laughter, and rising coffins force us to see the supernatural at work.

The decomposition of reality—which produces fantasy—is at the heart of *Passage from Home*. Bernard's desire to form a new family with Minna and Willy is related to his visions. The Passover Seder, which I have already mentioned, is full of fantasy: the light from the chandelier stains the wine, blurring everything at the table. Then "suddenly I saw myself walking in a broad field, not unlike the lawn in the park. . . . [At] my side was a young girl who shared the world with me, whose eyes danced and winked. . . . She was my aunt Minna, and yet not she. She was all girls in one, all mysteries and delightful things understood and possessed, and mine, all mine. . . ." Unlike the other writers, Rosenfeld gives us a wish-fulfillment dream here, but this eventually provokes anxiety because Bernard tries to shape reality to fit it. He is unsuccessful. Throughout his struggle he *sees* things. He stares at the fireplace in Minna's apartment—another "enlightenment"—and thinks of its fantastic qualities—fire is the "image of that raging, destructive spirit." He stares at old photographs which are "too oblique a version of the familiar." Gradually Bernard "lets go": reality and fantasy combine. He walks downtown, looking at the rushing crowds; he finds himself "alone, an object among objects, life among life, and the world—the very appearance of which asserted its intimate relationship to myself—was broken up into an unaccountable multiplicity without connection, just as bits of colored glass distributed at random in a kaleidoscope have no more in common than the external pattern that falls to them by chance." Reality becomes colored glass. Later, asleep in Minna's apartment—having achieved the "union" of the two adults—he begins to scratch his arm. He wakes and finds "a small, flat brown insect." The bedbugs—are they from Kafka?—assume symbolic value: they show him that he and the cot in which he sleeps are *unclean*. Dreams disturb Bernard. He dreams that he has become his father—his hair is gray, his eyes are *his* shape and color—and this occult phenomenon makes him think that he "had bridged the gulf between this life and the other." He has one more vision: as he gazes through the glass at the tropical plants in the hot-house—"high points of sun" attack him—he recognizes that he is now, for the first time, in touch with "the force common to all existence." He feels threatened and unwell—this, too, was in keeping with the "prevailing unnaturalness of the scene." The greenness is life's "vast, meaningless profusion"—that "blindness" has wrecked his plans for paternal knowledge. Bernard's last vision sends him back to his family—to the neat "white bed" (Schwartz' image).

Leslie Fiedler is very interested in fantasy. He admires the work of Nathaniel West, maintaining that he is "aware of a European tradition in thought and art, out of which Kafka, so like him in certain ways, had earlier emerged." Both West and Kafka have a "religious dimension" because they "are peculiarly apt at projecting images of numinous power for the unchurched." The last statement is especially important. Fiedler realizes that the "numinous power"—generated by the fusion of fantasy and realism—is a "modern" substitute for dogma. It is, in effect, our folk-religion. I take it that his admiration for Gothic American fiction—for such neglected writers as Hawkes, Barnes, and Henry Roth—lies in the fact that he sees their work as religious. Although he does not deal at length with *Passage from Home*, this novel surely confirms his belief: by using fantasy—nightmares and tipsy visions—Rosenfeld somehow introduces the numinous power of another world.

Fiedler's fiction attempts to do the same. (We have already seen the close relationship of his fiction and criticism.) It is not as successful as Rosenfeld's novel, but it does occasionally give us the ghostliness of existence.

"The Teeth" opens with these lines: "Children, dogs unnerved him. And the sun, inimical (he had forgotten his dark glasses, of course), found the narrow treeless gap of the street, his pale watery eyes." Heat and light conspire to unbalance Warren; he has the sense of "trespassing before each stoop." The world—nature, other people, and his own neurotic personality—is no longer "real" to him. In this story people assume ghostly qualities: it was a "boy, fourteen, perhaps fifteen, who leaned against the railing between sidewalk and house, resting; his mouth had dropped open and his unnoticed breath broke from it dog-like, *hunh! hunh! hunh!*" The boy limps after him, asking for a nickel. Who is he? Does he represent some "angel" or "demon"? Warren seems to regard him as his double. (The boy resembles the heavy bear, the dummy in Coney Island, and Shapiro's vulture.) When they quarrel, we are moved by sympathy: both are really half-alive. Later Warren reaches the apartment of his three female admirers, and he delights in shocking them by wearing play-teeth. These teeth are an amulet—a "supernatural" sign. Although Fiedler's hero is only *playing*, he realizes after his victory—the three women don't know what to do with him!—that he belongs to the teeth which, like Shapiro's Leg, master him. He cannot rid himself of his own grotesqueness. The story ends with "unseen laughter," darkness, and the "half-sleep of heat."

"The Fear of Innocence" gives us many fantastic details, which redeem its cliché—theme. The narrator, like Warren, enters foreign territory. "I came without music to the street, the house, the door; unsure, I waited while the bell made its catarrhal squawk in the imagined inner cube of dark and quiet." The inner cube introduces the idea of death, the unconscious, the other world. The narrator waits for Carrie to answer his ring. She does not. Now he tells us more about his reason for being here. He is "suspended," having just been freed from military service; he is seeking, as it were, on "the depthless glass his furtive image." (Remember Rosenfeld's symbolic glass.) He "moves" into the past—which is still depthless like the glass or the cube. He remembers that he was first drunk with Hal, his friend, and Carrie, their teacher. They were in Carrie's house (that unreal world so different from school), and their situation was completely "fantastic": Carrie, the straight-laced teacher, was Hal's sweetheart. The entire scene uses symbolic details to accentuate the fantasy—"I moved through the dark rooms from the door to my bed, kicking a chair in muddled resentment. . . . Meanwhile Hal (I thought dimly, falling, falling) was settled now into the female darkness of his fatherless house." Drunkenness represents the Fall into another world, "another dimension." More memories crowd him. He remembers Hal's deceptiveness, his use of "*my* name" in a list of actors. Identity is as dark as the inner cube. Is Hal dead or alive? Is Carrie dead or alive? Such questions plague the narrator who is haunted by their presence, even when, he now remembers, making love to his wife. When they tried to abort the fetus, birth and death merged fantastically. "I could not tell her my vision: the slow terror of being a child and the inevitable fall to hair, to awkwardness, to evil from that imbecile partial grace."

Ghosts come and go—until we are back in the present as he rings the bell. He waits. Finally he thinks that he smells death—the "abominable remnant of Carrie's flesh." He leaves the doorstep, afraid to open the door to that strangeness. He is not through yet. One more vision assaults him. He walks around the corner and sees a small girl bouncing a ball, "chanting in time to the throb of the rubber against the pavement, 'Bouncey, bouncey, ball-ee! I hope my sister fall-ee!'" Her face has a "dwarf's malice." The malice, the grotesqueness, the falling—these combine to startle the narrator who sees the terror of life. He runs, trying to escape, and he thinks of the Miltonic line, "Home to his mothers house private return'd." The line captures his ghostly life: the Mother is Carrie, his wife, the inner cube of darkness—death itself.

Ralph Freedman has discussed the change from *Dangling Man* to *The Adventures of Augie March* and *Henderson the Rain King*. "Although the reader still encountered familiar themes dealing with urban middle class life and urban squalor, he found them in unexpected contexts and configurations. Society was no longer only opposed to the hero, whether knowing or blind. Rather, it ironically reflected the hero's consciousness—functioning as his symbolic mirror—while at the same time it also maintained its time-honored place as the source and creator of his condition." [10] Mr. Freedman is correct in his discussion of the great change—a change so great that we marvel at how the same writer can give us *Henderson* and *Dangling Man*. But even in Bellow's early novels, as Mr. Freedman later suggests, "fantasy" combats reality, producing great tension.

A few dreams are found in *Dangling Man* after Joseph reaches the "edge of being." These represent his deep longings for punishment or escape from his plight. They occur because he can no longer suppress them. In one Joseph finds himself in a "low chamber with rows of large cribs or wicker bassinets in which the dead of a massacre were lying." He tells his dark guide that he must reclaim one of the bodies but, as an outsider, he doesn't know which one to choose. The other merely smiles at him and says, "It's well to put oneself in the clear in something like this." Then Joseph understands that he is searching for a special one. He continues to walk up the aisle:

> it was more like the path of a gray draught than anything so substantial as a floor. The bodies, as I have said, were lying in cribs, and looked remarkably infantile, their faces pinched and wounded. I do not remember much more. I can picture only the low-pitched, long room much like some of the rooms in the Industrial Museum in Jackson Park; the childlike bodies with pierced heads and limbs; my guide, brisk as a rat among his charges; an atmosphere of terror such as my father many years ago could conjure for me, describing Gehenna and the damned until I

shrieked and begged him to stop; and the syllables *Tanza.*

What does the dream mean? Joseph associates his present prison with the tomb—he is really looking for himself in one of the "large cribs." He is dead. But in a strange way he associates this death with childhood—the "childlike bodies"—as if he feels that his life ended before it began. There are two father figures: both are terrifying because they *know* about him; they don't offer any sympathy. Another aspect of the dream is Joseph's recognition of *damnation:* not only does he think that he is damned but he believes that his father has sentenced him here—indeed, the Vergil-like guide, the other father, reasserts the sentence, telling him to keep searching for his damned self in the crib. The dream, then, is fantastic, employing classic principles of condensation and displacement, but it describes underlying "reality"—Joseph's unconsciousness reasons for stasis.

Fantasy plays a bigger part in *The Victim*; it heralds the "complete" fantasy of *Henderson.* Here is one of Asa's dreams: He is on a boardwalk: the sea is on his right; on his left is an amusement park. He enters a hotel or store to buy rouge for Mary—inside is a "great, empty glitter of glass and metal." A girl demonstrates various shades, "wiping off each in turn with a soiled hand towel." This dream is comparatively "pleasant," but it is completely terrifying underneath. Asa wants desperately to buy a gift for his wife; he wants to please her because he needs her. Who is the salesgirl? Is she Mary or the whore Allbee has slept with in Asa's bed? Does Asa desire the girl? Why do the sea and the amusement park appear? All these questions are not easily answered, but they suggest that Asa's dream contains those elements—safety, normalcy, "transfer"—which he cannot really handle.

Now when we read *Henderson the Rain King*, we see that Bellow "lets go." The fantasy which occurred at crucial points in the early novels is completely in the foreground. The various rituals, gestures, and situations are, in effect, "waking dreams." "Africa" is the dark continent of the mind—anything can happen here: a dwarf can sit on a goddess; a man can "become" a lion; a ruler can speak in Reichian terms. Reality and fantasy are turned upside-down: fantasy is true reality; reality (of, say, Connecticut) is fantastic. Thus it is dangerous to ask all the time about *Henderson*: what does it mean? Fantasy implies intimations of meaning which cannot be "logically" grasped—as dreams are never really understood. Bellow is again fusing categories—because there is no such thing as reality in this novel, we are uncertain, plunged into the position of the hero who *wants* to know truth. As D. J. Hughes writes about *Lolita* and *Henderson the Rain King*: "in the novels under discussion, the reality which may exist beyond the wish-engendered fantasies of Humbert and Henderson is not at all clear. Their presumed insanity or abnormality does *not* lead us to a countering rational world; like their heroes, we must discover a reality through their wishes, and we must participate in their serious dreams. Only the excessively confident reader could do otherwise, and these novels are not written for confident readers. As a result, below the comic surface of each book, a desperate tone emerges, and a serious purgation takes place." [11]

Leslie Fielder has written about *The Assistant*, "It is odd how the subdued tone, the show of 'realism' in Malamud takes us in, as life itself takes us in, with its routine surfaces. We tend to accept on the level of mere realistic observation and reporting an account, say, of a young man wedged perilously in a dumbwaiter shaft watching the daughter of the man he has robbed but loves strip for a shower. (*No! in Thunder*)." Malamud, he tells us, gives us a "vision of the commonplace as absurd." Surely Fiedler is right—not only about *The Assistant* but about the short stories. Consider this description from "The Loan." "Screeching suddenly, [Bessie] ran into the rear and with a cry wrenched open the oven door. A cloud of smoke billowed out at her. The loaves in the trays were blackened bricks—charred corpses." The details seem realistic: a woman smells smoke and discovers that her loaves have burned. But notice the "cloud of smoke"—it becomes a "sign" of supernatural intervention. The burnt loaves have been "humanized" and then destroyed in a subtle way. The commonplace has been given fantastic life. Malamud doesn't stop here. He now describes the two friends. "Kobotsky and the baker embraced and sighed over their lost youth. They pressed mouths together and parted forever." In contrast to the "dead" loaves, the two men are still alive; they have enough vitality to sigh. But even they are touched by death: their youth is lost; they part forever. Malamud fuses the human and the "objective"—the baker and his bread—making reality a "visible legend"—to use Rosenfeld's phrase.

And he can go the other way. In a story like "Take Pity" he makes the fantastic commonplace. When we see Davidov, the census-taker, and Rosen, the ex-coffee salesman, in the "square, clean but cold room" we think they are just another pair of old men. Rosen complains a little—he doesn't need the shade up. Davidov takes out a pencil, sharpens it with an old blade, and proceeds to ask him questions. We sense now that there is something *different* about them. Rosen doesn't know his address; he doesn't know how to tell his story. Such details mount, and we realize finally that both are dead: Rosen has just killed himself to give Eva his money. Malamud is not interested in merely shocking us. His ghosts are, in effect, *still human*. After Davidov writes down the salesman's life in "an old-fashioned language" they don't use "nowadays," he raises the shade. Somehow Eva is there. This infuriates Rosen, who thinks that she had dared to die! "Go 'way from here. Go home to your children." Can she? The story ends as he pulls down the shade. We have been given a glimpse of the supernatural; we return to this world and wonder about our commonplace feelings.

It is possible to dislike such fantasy. Alfred Kazin has written that Malamud's people "talk to each other disbelievingly, as if each felt that the other was about to disappear, as if the world under their feet were itself unreal. [They] flit in and out of each other's lives like bad dreams." [12] Kazin recognizes that Malamud's fantasy is related to Jewish mysticism. "From the historic standpoint of Jewish theology, of the seemingly incredible Jewish experience itself, everything is entirely real. . . . In Malamud's stories everything real becomes unreal; we are under the sign not of theology but of surrealism." [13] But Malamud lapses into symbolic abstractness. Kazin thus misses in his work "a feeling for the value of life, for the body of this world—for that which cannot be explained because it is too precious to turn into symbols." [14] Of course, Kazin is correct about such stories as "Angel Levine" and "The Lady of the Lake," but he neglects to read Malamud closely. He does not explore details (such as those burnt loaves or the shade). These details do have "materiality." I think that the realistic *A New Life*, "A Choice of Profession," and "Black is My Favorite Color" (both from the recently published *Idiots First*) give us too much of this world's body.

They are less successful works. It is when Malamud is "suspended" between the sky and the ghetto that he is most effective; he is then ironic *and* fantastic.

In "Writing American Fiction," an essay which appeared in the March, 1961 issue of *Commentary*, Philip Roth writes, "the American writer . . . has his hands full in trying to understand, and then describe, and then make *credible* much of the American reality." This reality, he tells us, is "even a kind of embarrassment to one's own meager imagination." Although he does not plead for one kind of fiction, Roth seems to suggest that current novels should avoid conventional affirmation, "straight reportage." Obviously, if reality is so *unreal*, we need "off-center" vision and violent juxtapositions—fantastic art—to see ourselves clearly. But Roth is ambivalent. In his first novel, *Letting Go*, he wants to give us an analysis of contemporary America—one that reveals the dangers of "youthful unrealism"—to use Thomas Mann's phrase—which has caused the "sick joke" we are living. He does not know whether to use realism or fantasy. His three weaklings—Paul, Gabe, and Libby—are well-conceived (at least before their epiphanies)—sympathetic and ugly—but they don't incarnate the madness around us, unless Roth simply believes that such madness is caused by self-love. They are smart neurotics, not foolish fanatics—we see them every day. The need to expand his vision, to present a public commentary, forces Roth to add other characters—especially Martha, the widow, and her children (who adopt or are adopted by Gabe), and the former friends of Paul—whose endless conversations about child-rearing, modern furniture, and the often-depressing meaning of life are normal yet seem so out-of-place. This horizontal, trite enlargement is less effective than Roth's chilling vision of two minor characters who quarrel about the rights to boxes of underwear. These old men arrive on the scene to interrupt Paul and Libby. We see them briefly, but their fantastic being is, in the end, as memorable as the long-winded clichés of neurotics.

Roth's problem continues. His latest novel will deal with a suburban housewife. It will probably be as realistic as *Letting Go*. This loyalty to social realism is unfortunate. Roth is at his best in such fantastic art as Leo's bulb-visions ("Goodbye, Columbus"), Ozzie's leap, and Eli's change of clothing. Perhaps he has listened too eagerly to Alfred Kazin who, in reviewing *Goodbye, Columbus*, praised Neil Klugman's tone and, in general, the realistic picture of American society it conveyed. Such tone no longer helps us when American reality, as Roth himself has claimed, is so fantastic.

Our seven writers use fantasy in varying degrees. They give us ghosts, hallucinations, and nightmares because they accept the "extra-logicality" of life, although they do not believe in orthodox divinity. Their fantastic art is "a curious, almost uncanny transformation of the old Jewish mysticism [or folk-religion], where earth is so close to heaven—or to hell—that the supernatural and the trivial jostle each other. "Life is always strange and God always moves in unpredictable ways." [15]

"HOW IS IT CONCEIVABLE that the divine should be contained in such brittle vessels as consonants and vowels?" [1] asks Abraham Joshua Heschel. He answers poetically, "What else in the world is capable of bringing man and man together over the distances in space and in time? Of all things on earth, words alone never die. They have so little matter and so much meaning. . . . [It] is as if God took these Hebrew words and breathed into them of His power, and the words became a live wire charged with His spirit. To this very day they are hyphens between heaven and earth." [2] Perhaps the most important device found in the Bible is the parable—"a brief instructive story that, though it may concern some moral abstraction, remains as specific as the initial figure of speech." [3] The parable is "holiness in words" because it asserts, by its very form, the existence of universal meaning: it unites story and doctrine, the human and the divine, embodying harmonious relationships.

The desire to teach by means of "spiritual vocabulary"—Heschel's phrase—is a significant part of Jewish tradition. The Zohar, that strange work of mysticism, is a "parable of a parable," using the Biblical narrative to explain secret messages to the soul.

See how precisely balanced are the upper and lower worlds. Israel here below is balanced by the angels on high, concerning whom it stands written: "who makest thy angels into winds" [Psalms 104:4]. For when the angels descend to earth they don earthly garments, else they could neither abide in the world, nor could it bear to have them. But if this is so with the angels, then how much more so it must be with the Torah: the Torah it was that created the angels and created all the worlds and through Torah are all sustained.[4]

The line from Psalms is given flesh; it becomes the plot of another spiritual tale. This use of the parable extends into our "irreligious" century. Franz Kafka, for example, gives us another Zohar. When he confronts the story of Abraham and Isaac, he decides to rewrite it as a spiritual lesson (for himself?).

I could conceive of another Abraham—for myself— he certainly would have never gotten to be a patriarch or even an old-clothes dealer—who was prepared to satisfy the demand for a sacrifice immediately, with the promptness of a waiter, but was unable to bring it off because he could not get away, being indispensable; the household needed him, there was perpetually something or other to put in order, the house was never ready; for without having his house ready, without having something to fall back on, he could not leave—this the Bible also realized, for it says: "He set his house in order."[5]

Leslie Fiedler discusses Kafka's love of parable (or precept-tale).

From Esther and Jonah to the tales of the Hasidim, the haggadic method has survived in Jewry, the love of the story indistinguishable from the love of wisdom, the sense that what evades the precept flourishes in the tale. Kafka's comments on the Coming of the Messiah or the Tower of Babel might be the lost words of a *Zaddik*, at once a confession that some things are unsayable and that a Jew (why not?) can say them.

. . . Nor is Kafka's multivalence without ancestry; behind his devotion to the multiplicity of meaning lies the teaching that there are seventy true interpretations of each word of Scripture (*No! in Thunder*).

In Poems of a Jew Karl Shapiro gives us several narratives which, like Hasidic anecdotes or Kafka's parables, are spiritual lessons. "The Crucifix in the Filing Cabinet" is one of these. The narrator describes his "filing cabinet of true steel" which contains letters, bills, and contracts—his "trash of praise." He draws from it a crucifix, picking it up like a bird and placing it on his palm. Then he finds a "velvet bag" used by Jews to hold "holy shawls" and phylacteries. He drops the crucifix into the bag. The narrative is brief and instructive: it has taught us that Christian and Jew should live together—that there is no single religion which holds all truth. But is the tale simple? *How* does it instruct us? Shapiro—can we assume that he is the narrator?—uses symbolic associations and metaphoric language to establish the precept; the moral is *in* the narration. When he describes the filing cabinet as a steel receptacle for "all the trash of praise," it becomes more than a cabinet; it resembles a tomb, holding what "one acquires to prove and prove his days." But when one drawer rolls on "hidden wheels," and reveals the crucifix, the cabinet suddenly becomes a total mystery. The crucifix, unlike the inhuman (or dead?) cabinet, is alive—it is new, frightened-looking, and bird-like. When Shapiro describes it—like a "small mound of stones" on which an old tree stands, and on the tree some ancient teacher hangs—its light is almost divine. Then the "dark pouch" contains it. The union of the two objects is sacred: Shapiro does not tell us *when* the marriage takes place; he deliberately emphasizes the unique timelessness of the mysterious event, wanting us to see it "eternally."

Shapiro teaches us in "Adam and Eve" (a parable of

passion and intellect), "Messias," and other dramatic poems. "The Phenomenon" is less successful than these or "The Crucifix in the Filing Cabinet," but it does show us his general approach. He seems to begin with the precept—here it is "the world of the Nazis"—and then he constructs a tale which gives it life. *Idea comes first.* When Shapiro does find the right tale—as in "Adam and Eve" or "The Crucifix in the Filing Cabinet"—his poem is not irritatingly didactic. But occasionally he strains to incarnate his precepts. This is what happens in "The Phenomenon." Because he is so disturbed by the Nazis, he must get his lesson across. He represents Nazism as a "black snowfall," using symbolic language to emphasize the association—he gives us the clouds "fallen piecemeal into shrouds," the "obscurity of night." We are more aware of the precept than the tale; we cannot be moved by the many ingenious details. And when he finally delivers the message (a fairly obvious one), we are relieved.

It may seem ironic that Shapiro should write parables, especially since his recent conversion to Cosmic Consciousness. But this interest is not unexpected. He tries desperately, like ancient prophets, to re-educate the masses. Although he claims that he now writes "in defense of ignorance," he really wants them to learn from his experience. Thus he explains in his introduction to *Poems of a Jew* that "These poems are not for poets. They are for people who derive some strength of meaning from the writings of poets and who seek in the poet's mind some clue to their own thoughts. It is good to read poems for their own sake, but it is also good to read them as documents." The danger, which Shapiro does not avoid in some of his Jewish poems, is that the precept may inhibit poetic truth: documents are rather dull.

In "The World is a Wedding" Delmore Schwartz
gives us many parables (within one larger one). He
divides this short novel into ten sections; each section
uses a statement made by one of the characters as a
title. One: "What does she have that I don't have?"
Two: "How much money does he make?" Three: "No
one fools anyone much except himself." And so on.
The precept is given to us before the tale embodying
it. This short novel moves slowly because Schwartz is
less interested in narrative as such than in spiritual
lesson; but it does trace the "cosmic" effects of routine
actions and thoughts. Section Ten, headed by "The
best pleasure is to give us pleasure," demonstrates this
technique. We are told that the group of Jewish
intellectuals has changed (after the great depression).
Even Rudyard Bell, the center of the group, is ready to
move from New York to Cleveland. There is a farewell
dinner for him; afterwards his friends and his sister
discuss the future. There is little plot here. They talk;
they don't change the world. Schwartz uses their
discussions to emphasize their passivity. But at the
same time he knows that their precepts are powerful.
Ideas inform action. Section Ten really begins only
after the different characters offer us their lessons.
Laura, Rudyard's sister, tells a Kafka parable, distort-
ing it, but as she says, "I wrote the story from my
knowledge of life." She sees herself as the cow; Rudyard is the Siberian; and the others are the horses. The
Siberian and the horses devour her flesh. She teaches
them that she has nourished and sustained the group.
Marcus objects; so do some of the other "boys."
Laura continues her lesson, quoting in a slightly different context some of their previous precepts—these
hover over them. Now Jacob tells a parable to illus-
trate the Talmudic sentence he read recently. "The
world is a wedding." He uses Breughel's painting of

the wedding, finding in it different possibilities of humanity—"there are enough places and parts for everyone, and if no one can play every part, yet everyone can come to the party, everyone can come to the wedding feast." Laura contradicts him—for her "the world is a funeral." She ends the short novel by saying "Let me give all of you one good piece of advice: *Let your conscience be your bride.*"

Schwartz often employs a "center of consciousness." His narrator interprets action; he is *wed* to it. Thus even in his most "dramatic" tale, "In Dreams Begin Responsibilities," we find the same slow, reflective style as the narrator studies the *text* of his parents' courtship (as Laura examines Kafka or the Zohar examines Genesis), using the past event for spiritual lesson. Dramatic time—that is, plot or experience—is stopped so that it can become precept. Here is one example. The narrator informs us (and himself), "My father tells my mother how much money he has made in the past week, exaggerating an amount which need not have been exaggerated. But my father has always felt that actualities somehow fall short." He observes the past event, believing that it, like any other "simple" action, holds secret meaning. It instructs him about his father's lack of realism. The same technique is found in "Coriolanus and His Mother." The narrator seats us in a theatre where we watch a production of Coriolanus; he uses the play to teach us about "gross excess," pieties, and ethical action. Plot (on stage) is less important than precept. "Between the acts" the narrator himself takes the stage, giving us parables about the various themes of the play. He tells us about "Justice." "What could I think of, desiring to amuse as well as instruct, also to be pleased and to learn myself—of what but the ancient short story made known to me in childhood by my crippled father." This particular tale concerns a father and son and their "brown pony named Ego." Who is to ride the pony? Each does for a while. Then both ride at the same time. Then *they carry* the pony. Finally the father realizes the injustice of each action; unable to find a solution to the problem, he kills his son, Ego, and himself. The parable is not out of context; it is not a mere interlude. The "flat" characters, the simple action (or inaction), the many precepts and generalizations in it—all these inform Schwartz' complete fiction and poetry.

In an essay, "Mind, Body, Spirit: The Road to the Castle" Isaac Rosenfeld explains why he regards Hermann Hesse's *Magister Ludi* as "a book of wonders." He writes, "Hesse does not try to deduce characters from ideas, or vice versa, but dispenses with characterization altogether. Joseph Knecht, the hero, has the kind of existence that is given to philosophers by historians of culture: he stands at a point of intersection or convergence of lines of thought. . . . I kept waiting throughout the novel for something to happen; the usual conversion of character into drama. 'Nothing happens.' " (Hesse does the very thing that Schwartz does in "The World is a Wedding.") Rosenfeld's admiration for this novel (and for Kafka's parables) leads him to attempt the same unity in his fiction.

Although *Passage from Home* is a "dramatic" work, it depends less on plot than on reflection. Occasionally we sense that the characters are manipulated so that certain ideas can come forth. The Hasidic rabbi, the Gentile Willy, the bohemian Minna—all are "typical," standing for opposing values. Of course, the adolescent Bernard tends to judge adults for their abstract values; therefore we don't notice the manipulation as much here because, in a sense, it is psychologically motivated. Although the complete novel doesn't have the quality of parable, it does contain at least one long parable. Willy occupies the center of the stage. He offers a spiritual lesson as he narrates a childhood event. Once he ran away from home. He entered the dark woods. These events count less than the precepts they hold for him (and which he tries to give Bernard). About the flight through the woods he says, "You begin to feel that you've been on earth for a mighty long time. You forget this was all here before you and that it'll stand long after you're deep down under it." About his later adventures: "I had the feeling not only of being alone, but of being the only living creature left in the world." Willy cares less about plot than reflection, and his parable—really the one of the prodigal son (with variations)—captures his whole life. Bernard notes, "But I also felt that the story, and moreover the manner in which he had related it, established the theme of Willy's life." But is Willy's parable so different from Rosenfeld's technique in the entire novel? Doesn't *he* also care less about events than ideas *in* them? Isn't he trying to show that tales must instruct us?

Passage from Home is rather preachy because Rosenfeld is torn between "happening" and "nonhappening," drama and spiritual lesson. But in his later fiction, written after the Hesse essay, he tries to eliminate personality as such. He strips fiction until it becomes flat, simply plotted, and completely "instructive." I have already mentioned his parables of the clerk and the horse. In both we miss personality—the clerk embodies "clerkness"; the horse embodies horseness—we don't see individual difference. Indeed, when both creatures try to be different, they really falter. (There is, of course, a similarity here to Shapiro's use of abstractions in "The Phenomenon" or "The Convert" or Schwartz' pony, Ego). Rosenfeld tells us that he does not "begin with morality and look for a tale to clothe it—this procedure seems unnatural." The problem, in any event, is great and we must agree with him that true morality should be simple, obvious, and natural.

In his story, "The Brigadier" (*Partisan Review*, March–April, 1947), he does not step forth—as he does in *Passage from Home* or the formal dissertation on the clerk and horse. Here morality is simple and natural; it requires little "explanation." The unnamed narrator, the brigadier, looks after his captives, compiles intelligence reports, and wonders about the nature of the enemy. He is thoroughly involved with details; his thoughts about War arise out of his daily routine—consequently, we do not sense any *imposition* of spiritual truth. Truth lies in the brigadier's routine. When, for example, he tells us that "I work on the enemy proper. I am trying to discover what he is, what motivates him, what his nature is . . ." we accept the reality (and symbolism) of his statements. His routine subtly becomes our own, especially after he says, "The general had said that in certain respects we come to resemble the enemy. What are these respects? Perhaps the knowledge that I was seeking really lay in myself?" Rosenfeld is at his best in this story because he has found (unconsciously?) the perfect vehicle to instruct himself and us—one which does not push truth but, rather, asks us to pursue it along with the Brigadier—the parable of quest.

In his fiction Leslie Fiedler often begins with morality and grafts a tale onto it. This is what happens in *The Second Stone*. Clem, Hilda, and Mark Stone do not breathe; they are manipulated to teach us about Jews, Americans, and vanity—all of the dualities I have already discussed. They are burdened with

Truth. Donald Malcolm writes, "Every incident is neatly ticketed with its literary significance, and each character is furnished with a little handle by which the busy critic may grasp him and hold him up to the light, and shake him to hear how he rattles." [6] Malcolm is right about the didactic quality of this novel; but he does not realize that the novel fails because it attempts to be a "realistic" parable. The parable as a form seems to be successful only when it gives us a stylized and unreal world; it cannot describe social setting or details of personality. Thus if we compare *The Second Stone* and "The World is a Wedding" or "The Brigadier" we notice that Fiedler's precepts and narration never really fuse. Clem and Hilda seem to talk too much to be real people in Rome. Once we accept their *reality*—and the reality of their location—we see the clumsy unreality of their discussions. Fiedler instructs us more when he offers the stylized, fantastic detail—Clem's barking, Hilda's retching, or Mark's violent slapping of his wife. Perhaps I have simplified matters—the "real" Rome is also exaggerated. But it is still real enough—it has too much personality—to be an improper setting for parable.

Fiedler is at his best when he writes fantastic parables. In "The Dancing of Reb Hershl with the Withered Hand" we do not really see the "exceedingly prosperous Jewish community of M." or the eminent rabbis. Such description is less significant than the timeless conversations between the rabbis and Moshe; when they converse, they believe that *they* are being told. They embody eternal ideas, songs, parables, and proverbs. Because their existence presupposes divine wisdom, they are not as artificial as Hilda and Clem, when they try to "strike through the mask." Fiedler suggests in the last paragraph of this parable that the dancing of Reb Hershl is a "strange marriage" of "knowledge and bafflement," and his phrases can apply equally well to his theme. By using flat characters, stylized Talmudic debates, and sudden, inexplicable gestures (or visions), he demonstrates that precepts are always burdened with poetry. Thus he gives us prophecy, not the propaganda of *The Second Stone.*

In the preface to *An End to Innocence,* Fiedler tells us that "I do not mind, as some people apparently do, thinking of myself in . . . categorical terms; being representative of a class, a generation, a certain temper seems to me not at all a threat to my individuality. . . . I relish all that is typical, even me; and I like to think of myself as registering through my particular sensibility the plight of a whole group." His criticism resembles parable; through it he registers a "representative" temper. He not only views his own writing in this way; he regards a Whitman and James Jones—to mention only two writers—as representative—their work tells him the *truth* about our society, whether or not they think so. Because we do not understand his motives, we think that he may simply be over-ingenious. But if we relate his criticism to the tradition of the Zohar, the Talmud, and Kafka, we realize that "behind his devotion to the multiplicity of meaning lies the teaching that there are seventy true interpretations of each word of Scripture; and his obliquity evokes the Zohar's injunction that meaning should play lightly over the text, like the Spirit of the Lord hovering over the face of the waters" (*No! in Thunder* on Kafka). We may not agree with Fiedler at times—he may seem to be a propagandist—but his courageous interpretations are more valuable than "automatic" explication.

Saul Bellow does not give us a traditional parable like "The Dancing of Reb Hershl"—except perhaps for "Looking for Mr. Green"—but all of his novels assume, by their very structure, that personality cannot be separated from idea. Dialogue, reflection, and meditation dominate them; even when they employ description, the "real thing" is filtered through consciousness so that we always get multiplicity of meaning. Bellow's novels are, in effect, Talmudic exchanges. When the precepts are thrown at us without "playful" vision—as in some of Fiedler's essays or "The Phenomenon"—they irritate us. The conflict between preaching and prophecy is evident as theme and style in all of the novels. I want here to look at three.

In *The Victim* there are few artificial comments; the ideas arise dramatically. Bellow handles the dialogues about universal disorder with great care: Allbee, for example, bursts forth with such prophecies as "Hot stars and cold hearts, that's your universe." Perhaps the very fact that Schlossberg as moral guide must get his comments across makes him a "false" prophet—when he enters, we are ready for propaganda. Despite these minor flaws in prophetic dialogue, *The Victim* shakes us because of the unexpected, fantastic turns of phrase or idea.

We are so moved by Asa's unbalanced nature that when he has visions, we *know* them as we do not with Joseph in *Dangling Man*.

> We were all the time taking care of ourselves, laying up, storing up, watching out on this side and on that side, and at the same time running, running desperately, running as if in an egg race with the egg in a spoon. And sometimes we were fed up with the egg, sick of it, and at such a time would rather sign on with the devil and what they called the powers of darkness than run with the spoon, watching the egg, fearing for the egg.

The powers of darkness capture Asa. He is so involved that he cannot slow down; he must keep pace with his vision. Therefore he runs through his sentences (as does man with his egg). Perhaps Asa is less of a thinker than Joseph, responding more fearfully and quickly (as does the other when he sees the man fall). When he prophesies, we feel that his whole life—his very being—is at stake. He hasn't the energy to be theoretical.

The *Adventures of Augie March* is prophetic. At every point in the novel the hero vibrates to the "music of the spheres." When he gazes at the white and gray of Belguim, seeing himself as an *animal ridens* and Columbus, he captures the universal longings we all have; he is a "natural" visionary. But at other times, especially in the dialogues about truth and freedom, he is preaching to us. (Perhaps he is trying to convince himself.) When Augie explains his philosophy of the "axial lines of life," he is so involved with his language, his associations of thought, that he belabors a simple idea just to hear himself talk. Then he gives us explanation, not ecstasy. The novel is split between the two: the sudden, joyful insight into universal freedom, not the dull philosophy, is memorable. Augie is better "on the road."

One of the reasons for the split between preaching and prophecy is this: Augie is so enamored of his language—so "narcissistic"—that he cannot get out of himself. He lacks humility at times. It is, of course, dangerous to link Bellow with Augie, but the very fact that Joseph *and* Augie like to hear themselves talk means that involvement with self—can we call it preaching?—reappears because Bellow has not given up a vice. Often when Augie expounds his message, we are tempted to admonish him (and Bellow): *Get going.*

Fortunately Tommy Wilhelm does not have Augie's self-confidence. He cannot pursue a philosophical question at great length. Tommy Wilhelm *feels* things deeply—like Asa he is less intellectual than Joseph and Augie. He is a haunted man, always responding to the destructive world with dreams, fantasies, and visions. He prays suddenly. "Let me out of this clutch and into a different life. For I am all balled up. Have mercy." The desperate quality of his prayer demonstrates that he has no time for preaching.

Bellow juxtaposes the weak prophet to the preacher, Dr. Tamkin. The latter talks and talks; he even writes poems about his visions. Because of the tensions between the two men, we recognize basic separation of words and deeds. The split in *The Adventures of Augie March* is avoided—in fact, taken advantage of—by having two characters as "visionaries." When Dr. Tamkin speaks, we understand that he cannot *see*, although he would like to. "The interest of the pretender soul is the same as the interest of the social life, the society mechanism. This is the main tragedy of human life." Tommy recognizes himself *enacting* Tamkin's ideas; he *embodies* principles. Thus we are ready for complete prophecy when Tommy is away from the preacher and *stares at himself*. Not looking for universal truth, he finds it in his heart. "The flowers and lights fused ecstatically in Wilhelm's blind, wet eyes; the heavy sea-like music came up to his ears. It poured into him where he had hidden himself in the center of a crowd by the great and happy oblivion of tears. He heard it and sank deeper than sorrow, through torn sobs and cries toward the consummation of his heart's ultimate need."

Several critics have noted the parable-like quality of Malamud's short stories. Ben Siegel writes that they "deal primarily with contemporary Jewish life and represent the most consistent—if not the most 'realistic'—recent attempt to blend the traditional Yiddish folktale with the modern American scene and its values. Malamud most resembles such Yiddish masters as I. L. Peretz, Mocher Seforim, and Sholem Aleichem in his concern for morality and ethics rather than aesthetics." [7] Earl Rovit believes that this concern for morality cannot be separated from self-conscious craft: "His manner is frequently that of the teller of tales, but his technique of structure is poetic and symbolic." [8] In his best stories Malamud presents archetypal figures of traditional literature: the student, the simpleton, etc. He does not care very much about individual psychology. Leo Finkle, the rabbinical student of "The Magic Barrel"; Fidelman, the critic of "The Last Mohican"; Mitka, the writer-recluse of "The Girl of My Dreams"; the narrator of "The German Refugee"—all seem to blend into one character: the student of life. Of course, there are differences in their responses—some are more comical or more lonely—but they can easily switch places. They are used by Malamud to embody, if not personify, abstract innocence. Because they are "recurrent"—as are Fiedler's rabbis or Rosenfeld's Brigadier—they exist in a timeless world in which essence is more important than existence. We know, in effect, what will happen to them. (They also do.) No plot? No psychology? What then is left? Earl Rovit realizes that Malamud is concerned with the symbolic gesture, the text of life, not with "crude" happenings. "He seems, as it were, to construct his stories backwards—beginning with his final climactic image and then manipulating his characters into the appropriate dramatic poses which will contribute to the total significance of that image. . . . The dramatic action of the story attempts to lead the characters into a situation of conflict which is 'resolved' by being fixed poetically in the final ambiguity of conflicting forces frozen and united in their very opposition." [9] The image, the flat characterization, the frozen happening—have we not seen these in the best work of the other Jewish-American writers?

Malamud's problem is the novel. When he tries to broaden the range of his characters, making them normal or timely, he falters somewhat. In *A New Life* he wants to give a clear picture of contemporary society, a steady progression of events, and ideas of liberty and responsibility. He cannot. He fragments the novel. We remember the flat characters and symbolic gestures, not "didactic" Nature or the exchanges between Levin and faculty members. *The Assistant* is a better, more characteristic work because it possesses the qualities of parable—Siegel calls it a "parable of atonement and conversion" [10]—but it also is flawed. At times the characters, especially Helen and Frank, talk too much about the future. Their Talmudic dialogues are static. Again we remember the timeless, fantastic gestures—Frank's fall into the grave, his earlier rape—vision of nude Helen. In these lie poetic truth, not mere preaching. They resemble Asa's egg or Reb Hershl's dance.

Malamud is therefore at a crossroad. He can return to the fantastic parable of "The Magic Barrel"—as he does in *Idiot's First*—or try to explore "realistic parable." But as we have seen, the latter form, represented by *The Second Stone* and *The Adventures of Augie March*, is often unsuccessful. Malamud is trying to discover new forms (as well as tone), but his sense of structure is limited so far to poetic tableau. He has not yet given us anything as fresh (and yet as old) as "The World is a Wedding," in which flat description, saga-like time, and underlying precept become completely realistic. Can he break through?

Philip Roth asks the same question of himself. He is comfortable with the stylized madness of Eli and Ozzie; he does not have to individualize their crusades. By using "typical" figures—the student, the teacher, and the wandering Jew—he juxtaposes different ways of life. Occasionally his Eli and Ozzie are stereotypes, rather than archetypes—that is, their spiritual victories are easily gained. Unlike Malamud, Roth is also comfortable, too comfortable, with Fitzgerald-like realism. He can capture the normal Brenda Patimkin —her wisecracks, her diaphragm—problems. Even here he does not neglect his role as moralist, but he settles for low wisdom, undergraduate precepts.

Because he is torn by desire to write parable (as in "The Conversion of the Jews") and sophisticated realism (as in *Goodbye, Columbus*), he seeks a way out—a new technique. In *Letting Go* he regards himself as a teacher, warning us about the evils of obsessive (or innocent) benevolence. But he extends his lesson—or forgets it entirely—at times. It is significant that the novel begins and ends with letters. Roth resorts to these because he is unsure about our response to his wisdom. He wants to clarify the message. The letters—like the conversations of Hilda and Clem, the narcissistic meditations of Augie—seem out of place in a real world where wisdom rarely reaches the surface. Crude happening opposes essential learning in *Letting Go*.

Our seven writers want to communicate their spiritual lessons to us, but they are uncertain about the *shape* of wisdom. Should they write traditional parable? Should they subordinate event (or plot) to idea? Can they create new forms in which idea, happening, and personality are fully realized? These questions plague them. Often they take the easy way out—propaganda: they simply throw their messages at us as in *The Second Stone, Augie March, Letting Go,* or "The Phenomenon." But when they grapple with the tension between idea and happening (using it as theme and structure), they give us more than propaganda. In "The World is a Wedding," "Seize the Day," "The Brigadier" and "The Magic Barrel"—to cite only a few powerful works—they capture the poetic truth of parable. These works will endure because they incarnate our daily struggle between existence and essence, *how* and *why* we live. They are modern precept-tales.

CONTEMPORARY Jewish-American literature rebels against orthodoxy; it seeks some substitute faith— some new God. Such negativism offends many traditionalists, who ask for positive commitments, "affirmative" Jewishness. But as Leslie Fiedler and others have suggested, the "negativist is no nihilist": he affirms the existence of tradition, if only to battle it.

Despite their "open" rebelliousness our writers use (consciously or unconsciously) the traditional moments of Jewish Experience, translating these into modern terms. Their translation occasionally becomes distortion or inversion—nevertheless, it still assumes the glorious burden of Jewishness. The initial tension between orthodoxy and non-commitment is constantly "reaffirmed." When our writers deal with head and heart, fathers and sons etc., they think dualistically. Their works assert that the Jew starts with tension and never finds complete relief. Even their literary devices—irony, fantasy, and parable—embody dualities:

The American Jew often finds that his peculiar tensions alienate him from the larger community. While trying to resolve his feelings about the Jewish Past, for example, he must confront another myth which assumes that the present is all-important. Each thematic moment of Jewish Experience is somewhat alien to Gentile Americans. The American Jew, in other words, is unsure of his Jewish and American commitments. He is a "specialist in alienation."

The irony of the situation lies in the fact that such parochial tensions are "universal." Now non-Jew *and* Jew live in the "age of anxiety"; by rendering their private feelings, our writers appeal to Gentile readers in Fort Wayne or Paris. Malamud has said "All men are Jews." Perhaps he is right in a metaphoric way.

I think that when our writers are at their best, they clearly express their tensions without indulging in Old World charm or self-pity. They can never be as popular as those "inauthentic" Jews who produce bestsellers about World War II or Central Park West by avoiding negativism. When our writers flee from tension into easy Transcendence—Reichian joy, Nature etc.—they seem as false as these popularizers.

Can't Jewishness be found in any book about Jewish life? Must it exist only in spiritual moments? Must it be tense? Such questions take us to the heart of the matter: Jewish-American literature must start with traditional moments and transform them; it must assert the "supernatural," even if it finally claims that divinity no longer exists. It must profoundly shock us. *The Victim*, "The Crucifix in the Filing Cabinet," *The Assistant*, "The World is a Wedding"—these works, among others, disturb us because they rebel against (and paradoxically *affirm*) spiritual moments. They create—and are created by—fear and trembling. Fiedler's words about Simone Weil apply as well to the "unbalanced," complex affirmation of Jewish-American writers. "To those who consider themselves on the safe side of belief, [they] teach the uncomfortable truth that the belief of many atheists is closer to a true love of God and a true sense of his nature, than the kind of easy faith which, never having *experienced* God, hangs a label bearing his name on some childish fantasy." [1] The Jewish Experience is great enough to accept our rebellious writers.

1 — Introduction

1. Leslie Fiedler, "On the Road; or the Adventures of Karl Shapiro," *Poetry*, XCVI, 171.

2. "A Vocal Group," *TLS*, November 6, 1959, p. xxxv.

3. Fiedler, *op. cit.*, 171.

4. Theodore Solotaroff, "Harry Golden and the American Audience," *Commentary*, XXXI, 8.

5. Arthur A. Cohen, *The Natural and Supernatural Jew* (New York: Pantheon, 1963), offers a valuable discussion of the loss of supernatural "vocation" by the American Jew. There are several studies of the American Jew: *The Jews* (ed.) Marshall Sklare, *Protestant-Catholic-Jew* by Will Herberg, and *American Judaism* by Nathan Glazer — to mention only three.

6. Paul Lauter, "The Jewish Hero: Two Views," *The New Republic*, November 24, 1958, pp. 18–19.

7. His comments, on pp. 12–14, are part of a symposium on the Jewish writer in America.

8. Cf. Theodore Solotaroff's introduction to *An Age of Enormity: Life and Writing in the Forties and Fifties* (Cleveland and New York: World, 1962), a selection of Rosenfeld's essays. I will refer in a later chapter to the relation of Reich to the Hasidic Masters.

9. Quoted on the jacket of *Pull Down Vanity* published by J. B. Lippincott.

10. I assume that the Viking notes are supplied by Bellow.

11. Earl H. Rovit, "Bernard Malamud and the Jewish Literary Tradition," *Critique*, III, No. 2 (Winter, Summer, 1960), p. 5.

12. Jean-Paul Sartre, *Anti-Semite and Jew* (New York: Evergreen Books, 1960), p. 67.

13. Arthur A. Cohen, "Why I Choose To Be a Jew," *Harper's*, April, 1959, p. 61.

14. Abraham Joshua Heschel, *God in Search of Man* (New York: Meridian Books, 1959), p. 131. I am deeply indebted to this book for its profound interpretation of Jewishness.

15. Will Herberg, *Judaism and Modern Man* (New York: Meridian Books, 1959), p. 25.

16. Heschel, p. 244.

2 – *Exile*

1. Arthur Hertzberg (ed.), *Judaism* (New York: Washington Square Press, 1963), p. 140.

2. *Ibid.*, p. 159. *The Reconstructionist*, founded by Mordecai Kaplan, frequently contains articles on this question.

3. Herberg, *Judaism and Modern Man*, p. 275.

4. Cf. Arnold A. Rogow (ed.), *The Jew in a Gentile World* (New York: Macmillan, 1961), pp. 219–373, for selections on "The Jew in America." Edmund Wilson's discussion of "Judaistic" thinking in Puritan New England is included.

5. Morse Peckham, *Beyond the Tragic Vision* (New York: Braziller, 1962), pp. 42–43.

6. Rovit, "Bernard Malamud and Jewish Literary Tradition," p. 8.

7. Saul Bellow's review of *Goodbye, Columbus* is entitled "The Swamp of Prosperity" (*Commentary*, XXVIII, 77–79).

8. *Ibid.*, 77.

9. *Ibid.*, 78.

3—*Fathers and Sons*

1. Hertzberg, *Judaism*, p. 86.
2. *Ibid.*, p. 88.
3. *Ibid.*
4. Louis I. Newman (ed.), *The Hasidic Anthology* (New York: Schocken Books, 1963), p. 155.
5. Herberg, *Judaism and Modern Man*, p. 79.
6. *Ibid.*
7. *Ibid.*, p. 80.
8. *Ibid.*, p. 81.
9. Cf. Albert I. Gordon, "The Jewish Family," *Jews in Suburbia* (Boston: Beacon Press, 1959), pp. 57–85, for a sociological picture.
10. Geoffrey Gorer, *The Americans* (London: Grey Arrow Books, 1959), pp. 28–29.
11. Cf. Earl H. Rovit, "Fathers and Sons in American Fiction," *Yale Review*, LIII, for an interesting discussion of the subject.
12. Heinz Politzer, "Two Worlds of Delmore Schwartz," *Commentary*, X, 562.
13. Cf. Martha Wolfenstein, "Two Types of Jewish Mothers," in Marshall Sklare (ed), *The Jews* (Glencoe, Illinois: Free Press, 1958), pp. 520–35, for a brilliant psychological study of Old and New World mothers.
14. Solotaroff, "Introduction," p. 30.
15. Benjamin De Mott, *Hells and Benefits* (New York: Basic Books, 1962), p. 203.
16. Richard Chase, "The Adventures of Saul Bellow," *Commentary*, XXVII, 330.
17. Jonathan Baumbach, "The Economy of Love: The Novels of Bernard Malamud," *Kenyon Review*, XCVIII, 456.

4—*Time*

1. Heschel, *God in Search of Man*, p. 200.
2. *Ibid.*, p. 205.
3. Hertzberg, *Judaism*, p. 1.

4. R. W. B. Lewis, *The American Adam: Innocence, Tragedy and Tradition in the Nineteenth Century* (Chicago: University of Chicago Press, 1955), pp. 45–46.

5. The phrase is Mr. Lewis'.

6. Herberg, *Judaism and Modern Man*, p. 201.

7. Politzer, "Two World of Delmore Schwartz," 563.

5—Head and Heart

1. Heschel, *God in Search of Man*, p. 341.

2. Nahum N. Glatzer (ed.), *A Jewish Reader* (New York: Schocken Books, 1961), p. 135.

3. *Ibid.*, p. 127.

4. Hanan J. Ayalti (ed.), *Yiddish Proverbs* (New York: Schocken Books, 1963), p. 117.

5. *Ibid.*, p. 115.

6. *Ibid.*, p. 59.

7. Glatzer, p. 86.

8. Heschel, p. 20.

9. *Ibid.*, p. 19.

10. Glatzer, p. 100.

11. Heschel, p. 20.

12. Shapiro tells us that the poem's imagery is based on the *Zohar* and the work of Wilhelm Reich.

13. Cf. Theodore Solotaroff, "The Irrational Karl Shapiro," *Commentary*, XXX, 445–49, for a valuable discussion of Shapiro's "irrationalism" in relation to the recent work of Bellow, Mailer, Lowell and Roethke.

14. Politzer, "Two Worlds of Delmore Schwartz," 561.

15. Solotaroff "Introduction," pp. 38–39.

16. *Ibid.*, p. 16.

17. De Mott, *Hells and Benefits*, p. 198.

18. *Ibid.*

19. Cf. his discussion in *New York Times Book Review*, September 20, 1953, p. 1.

20. Robert Penn Warren, "Man with No Commitments," *New Republic*, November 2, 1953, p. 23.

21. Chester Eisinger, "Saul Bellow: Love and Identity," *Accent*, XVIII, 193.

22. Edmund Bergler, "Writers of Half-Talent," *American Imago*, XIV, 155.

6—Transcendence

1. Heschel, *God in Search of Man*, p. 29.
2. *Ibid.*, p. 31.
3. *Ibid.*
4. Cf. Heschel's discussion of "Wonder," "The Sense of Mystery," "The Sublime," and "Awe."
5. Heschel, p. 43.
6. Robert W. Flint, "The Stories of Delmore Schwartz," *Commentary*, XXXIII, 337.
7. Irving Howe, "Delmore Schwartz—A Personal Appreciation," *New Republic*, March 19, 1962, p. 27.
8. Rosenfeld's statement is related to Norman Mailer's in "The White Negro": "our collective condition is to live with instant death." It is interesting to note that Mailer has recently turned to the Hasidic Masters (as interpreted by Martin Buber). There is a subtle chain which links Hasidism, Reichianism and Hipsterism—all three "styles of life" seek Joy.
9. Solotaroff, "Introduction," p. 28.
10. Wilhelm Reich, *Selected Writings: An Introduction to Orgonomy* (New York: Noonday Press, 1961), p. 146.
11. *Ibid.*, p. 151. Cf. the definition of "neurotic character" as given in the glossary: "The character which, due to chronic bioenergetic statis operates according to the policy of compulsive moral regulation" (p. 10).

7—Irony

1. Israel Knox, "The Traditional Roots of Jewish Humor," *Judaism*, XII, 327–37.
2. *Ibid.*, p. 331.
3. *Ibid.*, pp. 331–32.
4. Franz, Kafka, *Parables and Paradoxes* (New York: Schocken, 1961), p. 93.

5. Knox, p. 329.

6. Politzer, "Two Worlds of Delmore Schwartz," 562.

7. *Ibid.*, p. 568.

8. Knox, p. 334.

8 — *Fantasy*

1. Solotaroff, "Introduction," p. 25.

2. Joshua Trachtenberg, *Jewish Magic and Superstition* (New York: Meridian Books, 1963), p. vii.

3. *Ibid.*, p. 187.

4. *Ibid.*, p. 239.

5. *Ibid.*, p. 230.

6. Richard Chase, *The American Novel and Its Tradition* (New York: Anchor Books, 1957), pp. 1–2.

7. Leon Edel, "Introduction," *Ghostly Tales of Henry James* (New York: Universal Library, 1963), pp. vii–viii.

8. *Ibid.*, p. viii.

9. Trachtenberg, pp. 78–104.

10. Ralph Freedman, "Saul Bellow: The Illusion of Environment," *Wisconsin Studies in Contemporary Literature*, I, 51.

11. D. J. Hughes, "Reality and the Hero: 'Lolita' and 'Henderson the Rain King,'" *Modern Fiction Studies*, VI, 348–49.

12. Alfred Kazin, "Bernard Malamud: The Magic and the Dread," *Contemporaries* (Boston: Little, Brown — Atlantic Monthly Press, 1962), p. 205.

13. *Ibid.*

14. *Ibid.*, p. 207.

15. *Ibid.*, p. 205.

9 — *Parable*

1. Heschel, *God in Search of Man*, p. 244.

2. *Ibid.*

3. Harold H. Watts, *The Modern Reader's Guide to the Bible* (New York: Harper, 1959), p. 207. Cf. his dis-

cussion of the relation between parable and metaphor on the same page.

4. Gershom G. Scholem (ed.), *Zohar: the Book of Splendor* (New York: Schocken Books, 1963), p. 121.

5. Kafka, *Parables and Paradoxes*, p. 41.

6. Donald Malcolm, "Much Ado," *The New Yorker*, August 17, 1963, p. 84.

7. Ben Siegel, "Victims in Motion: Bernard Malamud's Sad and Bitter Clowns," *Recent American Fiction*, ed. Joseph J. Waldmeir (Boston: Houghton Mifflin, 1963), pp. 204–5.

8. Rovit, "Bernard Malamud and the Jewish Literary Tradition," pp. 5–6.

9. *Ibid.*, p. 6.

10. Siegel, "Victims in Motion," p. 205.

10—Postcript

1. Leslie Fiedler, "Introduction," *Waiting for God* by Simone Weil (New York: Capricorn Books, 1959), p. 5.

INDEX